Altered PASTS

Altered PASTS

COUNTERFACTUALS IN HISTORY

RICHARD J. EVANS

THE MENAHEM STERN JERUSALEM LECTURES

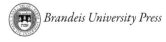 *Brandeis University Press*  *Historical Society of Israel*

BRANDEIS UNIVERSITY PRESS Waltham, Massachusetts

BRANDEIS UNIVERSITY PRESS / HISTORICAL SOCIETY OF ISRAEL

An imprint of University Press of New England

www.upne.com

© 2013 Richard J. Evans

Manufactured in the United States of America

Designed by Richard Hendel

Typeset in Garamond Premier Pro by Tseng Information Systems, Inc.

University Press of New England is a member of the Green Press Initiative.
The paper used in this book meets their minimum requirement for recycled
paper.

For permission to reproduce any of the material in this book,
contact Permissions, University Press of New England, One Court Street,
Suite 250, Lebanon NH 03766; or visit www.upne.com

Library of Congress Cataloging-in-Publication Data

Evans, Richard J.

Altered pasts: counterfactuals in history / Richard J. Evans.

  pages cm. — (The Menahem Stern Jerusalem lectures)

Includes bibliographical references and index.

ISBN 978-1-61168-537-4 (cloth: alk. paper) — ISBN 978-1-61168-538-1 (pbk.: alk.
paper) — ISBN 978-1-61168-539-8 (ebook)

1. Imaginary histories. 2. History — Philosophy. 3. Historiography — Political
aspects — Great Britain. 4. Great Britain — History — 20th century. 5. Right and
left (Political science) — Great Britain. I. Title.

D21.3.E87 2013

901 — dc23

2013029719

5 4 3 2 1

FOR CHRISTINE

If we had not met . . .

The historian . . . must always maintain towards his subject an indeterminist point of view. He must constantly put himself at a point in the past at which the known factors still seem to permit different outcomes. If he speaks of Salamis, then it must be as if the Persians might still win; if he speaks of the coup d'état *of Brumaire then it must remain to be seen if Bonaparte will be ignominiously repulsed. . . . [Yet] the historian tries to discover some sense in the remains of a certain period in human society. . . . The historical context we posit, the creation of our mind, has sense only insofar as we grant it a goal, or rather a course towards a specific outcome. . . . Therefore historical thinking is always teleological. . . . For history the question is always "Whither?" History must be granted to be the teleologically oriented discipline* par excellence.

—JOHAN HUIZINGA, quoted in Fritz Stern, ed.,
  The Varieties of History: From Voltaire to the Present

CONTENTS

FOREWORD

The following pages reproduce, with additions, the Menahem Stern Jerusalem Lectures that Richard J. Evans delivered in April, 2013. Before coming to Cambridge, where he has been professor of modern history, Regius Professor of History, and president of Wolfson College, he had taught at Stirling, East Anglia, Columbia, and Birkbeck College, London. He is a Fellow of the British Academy, of the Royal Historical Society, and of the Royal Society of Literature, and a regular broadcaster and writer for the literary and political press. His 1987 book *Death in Hamburg* is a prize-winning history of the 1892 cholera epidemic, which reconstructs not only what had happened but also the state of medical science at the time, the social services, the class inequalities, and many other relevant themes. This book was the basis for a German film televised in 1990. In the Lipstadt-Irving trial in 2000, Professor Evans was the main witness for Lipstadt, who as defendant was vindicated.

Richard J. Evans is first and foremost a historian of Germany. He not only contributed to it numerous studies, but he also opened up fields of German history that had been mostly neglected before. Led by his interest in history from below, he pioneered such new fields as German feminism, the working classes, crime and punishment, medicine and disease, labor and the peasantry, the proletariat, the underworld, and the unemployed. His research included the juridical system, torture, witchcraft, forms of execution, social conditions and relations, family life. On all of these subjects and more, he conducted pioneering research and built up new schools of thought. He is interested in both central and marginal parts of society, in outcasts as well as political leaders. His book *Rituals of Retribution* traces the history of capital punishment in Germany over centuries, not just as an instrument of the law but also as a form of state power. And all of these seemingly specialized subjects are shown to be essential for a full understanding of the German social and political culture, including the acceptance of authoritarian regimes, as well as the activities of organizations from below.

His trilogy on the Nazi period has been generally recognized as the definitive history of that period. *The Coming of the Third Reich*, *The Third Reich in Power*, and *The Third Reich at War* were published between 2003 and 2008. Of special interest are the thematic chapters dealing with the different aspects of public life, such as education, the press, the cinema, the economy, the universities, and many other aspects, each researched and presented with great expertise and detail, in its own professional terms. The combination of analysis and integration, policies and processes, conscious decisions and emotional reactions effectively brings the period to life.

Careful and critical examination of other historians' work or mistakes has rightly become an essential part of history writing. The value of this approach is brought out in Richard J. Evans's works of historiographical analysis, which include *In Hitler's Shadow*, a sharp-sighted book on the *Historikerstreit* of the 1980s, which has other historians' arguments as its central theme. In his book *In Defense of History* (1997) we find his most interesting approach to causality in history, which is clearly nondeterministic. He argues that Nazism was not, in his opinion, an inevitable result of German traits, even though one can show certain continuities. The failure of the liberal revolutions of 1848 did not cause the rise of Nazism. The Sonderweg was not an inevitable development. There were other possibilities, and there is almost invariably more than one historical explanation of why a certain road was taken and others were not. In his most recent book, *Cosmopolitan Islanders*, he studies the engagement of British historians with the European past. The present short book falls into this series, as a study of mainly British, and to some extent also American, French, German, and Italian, studies of "what-if" questions in history. It analyzes specific examples of this approach, particularly in relation to twentieth-century Germany, as well as the epistemological problems raised by "counterfactual" history.

HEDVA BEN-ISRAEL
Hebrew University Jerusalem

PREFACE

This short book is an essay on the use of counterfactuals in historical research and writing. By counterfactuals, I mean alternative versions of the past in which one alteration in the timeline leads to a different outcome from the one we know actually occurred. In the chapters that follow, examples that are discussed at length include what would have happened had Britain not entered the First World War but stood aside as a neutral nonbelligerent; what the result might have been had Britain concluded a separate peace with Nazi Germany in 1940 or 1941; or how the British might have behaved had they lost the Battle of Britain and been conquered and occupied by the armed forces of Hitler's Third Reich. The opening chapter surveys the development of counterfactual history from its beginnings in the nineteenth century, and tries to account for its revival and its popularity, especially in Britain and the United States, in the 1990s and 2000s. The second considers the arguments for and against the use of counterfactuals, and discusses some of the principal contributions to the genre and their implications for what many of their authors call historical determinism. Chapter 3 looks at a variety of ways in which writers of history and fiction have reinvented the past for their own purposes, including the construction of parallel "alternate" histories and imaginary representations of the future based on alterations made to the past. The fourth and final chapter tries to pull all this together and reach some kind of conclusion about whether or not counterfactuals are a useful tool for the historian, and, if so, in what ways, to what extent, and with what limitations.

I first became interested in counterfactuals in 1998, when I took part in a televised discussion on BBC News 24's program *Robin Day's Book Talk* with Antonia Fraser and Niall Ferguson, who had just published his pathbreaking book in the field, *Virtual History*. My own *In Defense of History* had just come out, and the idea of counterfactual history seemed to raise in a new way the fundamental questions about the borders between fact and fiction with which that book had tried to grapple. So when I was asked to deliver the Butterfield Lecture at Queen's University, Belfast, in October 2002, it seemed a good opportunity to come to grips with these questions at greater length. An edited version of the lecture was published as "Telling It Like It Wasn't," in the *BBC History Magazine*, number 3 (2002), pp. 2–4; and then reprinted by request in the American journal *Historically Speaking*, issue 5/4 (March 2004), where it was the subject of several lively and lengthy discussions, to which I was able to reply in the same issue (pp. 28–31); the whole exchange was reprinted in Donald A. Yerxa's *Recent Themes in Historical Thinking: Historians in Conversation* (Columbia, SC: University of South Carolina Press, 2008), pp. 120–30.

The response by Geoffrey Parker and Philip Tetlock in *Historically Speaking*, and the more elaborate arguments they deployed in the introduction and conclusion to their edited volume of counterfactuals, *Unmaking the West*, published two years later, made me realize that my initial, somewhat allergic reaction to the claims made by the counterfactualists needed rethinking, and the appearance in the following years of further contributions to the genre gave me further cause for reconsideration. Moreover, there are by now several theoretical and reflective considerations of the problems counterfactual history raises, ranging from the highly critical to the carefully justificatory. These have helped move the debate to a new level. So when I was asked by the Historical Society of Israel, an independent organization whose history goes back well into the 1930s, to deliver the Menahem Stern Jerusalem Lectures for 2013 on some topic of historical interest with a particular emphasis on its methodological and theoretical aspects, I welcomed the opportunity to revisit the subject of counterfactuals and think about it at further length. The present book is the result. It reprints the lectures more or less as given, except that chapters 3 and 4 were merged and abridged to form the third and final lecture in the series, and some material and arguments have subsequently been added to the text.

My first debt of gratitude is to the Historical Society of Israel, its chairman, Professor Israel Bartel, its general secretary Mr. Zvi Yekutiel, and its board of directors for having done me the signal honor of inviting me to give the lectures. Following in the footsteps of historians such as Carlo Ginzburg, Anthony Grafton, Emmanuel Le Roy Ladurie, Fergus Millar, Natalie Zemon Davis, Anthony Smith, Peter Brown, Jürgen Kocka, Keith Thomas, Heinz Schlling, Hans-Ulrich Wehler, and Patrick Geary is a daunting task, but it was made easier for me by Maayan Avineri-Rebhun, the society's academic secretary, who arranged everything with exemplary courtesy and efficiency. Tovi Weiss provided indispensable assistance, and the staff at Mishkenot Sha'ananim, the guesthouse and cultural center on the hill overlooking the forbidding walls of the Old City of Jerusalem, were unfailingly helpful. The audiences who listened patiently to the lectures helped improve the book's arguments with their questions, while Otto Dov Kulka not only pointed me toward the thought of Johan Huizinga on this topic but also proved a genial and stimulating host in our travels in and around Jerusalem, where Ya'ad Biran provided expert guidance around the endlessly fascinating sites to be found within the city walls. Professor Yosef Kaplan, chief editor of the Stern Lecture Series, helped see the lectures into print. My agent, Andrew Wylie, and his staff, especially James Pullen at the London branch of the agency, worked hard to secure the book's publication under terms that will, it is to be hoped, give it a wide distribution. The staff at Brandeis University Press were thorough and professional, and I am particularly grateful to Richard Pult and Susan Abel, for overseeing the production process, to Cannon Labrie for his expert copyediting of the typescript, and to Tim Whiting at Little, Brown, for his work on the UK and Commonwealth edition. Simon Blackburn,

Christian Goeschel, Rachel Hoffman, David Motadel, Pernille Røge, and Astrid Swenson read the typescript on short notice and suggested many improvements. Christine L. Corton cast an expert eye over the proofs. I am grateful to them all, though none of them bears any responsibility for what follows.

RICHARD J. EVANS
Cambridge
July 2013

Altered PASTS

CHAPTER 1 *Wishful Thinking*

What if? What if Hitler had died in a car crash in 1930: Would the Nazis have come to power, would the Second World War have happened, would six million Jews have been exterminated? What if there had been no American Revolution in the eighteenth century: Would slavery have been abolished earlier, and the Civil War of 1860–65 have been avoided? What if Balfour had not signed his declaration: Would the state of Israel have come into being at all? What if Lenin had not died in his early fifties but survived another twenty years: Would the murderous cruelties of what became the Stalin era have been avoided? What if the Spanish Armada had succeeded in invading and conquering England: Would the country have become Catholic again, and if so, what would have been the consequences for art, culture, society, science, the economy? What if Al Gore had won the American presidential election in the year 2000: Would there have been a Second Gulf War? What if — as Victor Hugo speculated at enormous length in his enormous novel *Les Misérables* — Napoleon had won the Battle of Waterloo? How indeed, the novelist asked in bewilderment, could he possibly have lost? [1] Things that happened, as James Joyce wrote in *Ulysses*, "are not to be thought away. Time has branded them and fettered they are lodged in the room of the infinite possibilities they have ousted. But can those have been possible seeing that they never were? Or was that only possible which came to pass?" [2]

The question of what might have happened has always fascinated historians, but for a long time it fascinated them, as E. H. Carr observed in his *What Is History?*, his Trevelyan Lectures at Cambridge in 1961, as nothing more than an entertaining parlor game, an amusing speculation of the sort memorably satirized centuries ago by Pascal, when he asked what might have happened had Cleopatra had a smaller nose, and therefore not been beautiful, and so not proved a fatal attraction to Mark Antony when he should have been preparing to defeat Octavian, thus causing him to lose the Battle of Actium. Would the Roman Empire never have been created?[3] Most likely it would, even if in a different way and possibly at a slightly different time. Larger forces were at work than one man's infatuation. Similar satirical intent can be found in the eighteenth century, in popular stories such as *The Adventures of Robert Chevalier*, published in 1732 in Paris and quickly translated into English, which imagined the Native Americans discovering Europe before the voyages of Columbus.[4] And, famously, Edward Gibbon, in his *History of the Decline and Fall of the Roman Empire* poked fun at the university in which he had spent what he called the most idle, and the most unprofitable years of his life, by suggesting that if Charles Martel had not defeated the Moors in 733, Islam might have dominated Europe and "perhaps the interpretations of the Koran would now be taught in the schools of Oxford, and her pulpits might demonstrate to a circumcised people the sanctity and truth of the revelation of Mohammed."[5] Clearly Gibbon thought that in the end, at least as far as Oxford was concerned, things would have been much the same as they were.

Brief allusions to possible alternatives to what actually happened can be found scattered across the works of a variety of authors through the centuries, from the Roman historian Livy's speculation on what might have happened had Alexander the Great conquered Rome, to Joanot Martorelli and Martí Joan de Galba's 1490 romance *Tirant lo Blanc*, which imagined a world in which the Byzantine Empire defeated the Ottoman Empire and not the other way around. Written within a few decades of the actual fall of Constantinople to the Turks, it was the first approach to a fantasy history to appear, and had a clear element of wishful thinking in it. Yet it had no real followers for a very long time. A rationalistic approach to history such as Gibbon's, replacing a view of the human past that treated it as the unfolding of God's Divine Providence in the world, was an essential prerequisite for speculating at length in historical rather than fictional writing on possible alternatives to what happened. As Isaac D'Israeli pointed out in 1835 in the first treatment of the subject, a brief essay entitled "Of a History of Events Which Have Not Happened," the concept of Divine Providence could not convince an impartial observer when both Protestants and Catholics claimed it for their own. This insight was not new, though D'Israeli tried to buttress it by mentioning a number of historical texts that speculated, even if only very briefly, on what might have happened had, for example, Charles Martel lost to the Moors, the Spanish Armada landed in England, or Charles I not been executed. All D'Israeli really wanted to argue was that historians should replace the idea of "Providence" with the concepts of "fatality," as he called it, and "accident."[6] Yet one further step was needed before such speculations could be unfolded at length. Gibbon, like other Enlightenment historians, still regarded time as unchanging and human society as static: his Roman senators can easily be imagined as bewigged eighteenth-century gentlemen debating in the House of Commons, and the moral qualities they displayed were much the same as Gibbon found among his contemporaries. It required the new Romantic vision of the past as essentially different from the present, with each epoch possessing its own peculiar character, as the novelist Walter Scott and his historical disciple Leopold von Ranke believed, for the question of how the principal characteristics of an era might have been dramatically altered if history had taken a different course.[7]

Unsurprisingly, it was a French admirer of the emperor Napoleon, Louis Geoffroy, who first developed this idea at length. Indeed, the emperor himself spent a good deal of his time on the island of St. Helena, where he had been exiled following his defeat at Waterloo, in dreaming about how he might have defeated his enemies. If the Russians had not set fire to Moscow as the Grand Army neared its gates in 1812, he sighed, his forces could have overwintered in the city, then, "as soon as good weather returned, I would have marched on my enemies; I would have defeated them; I would have become master of their empire . . . for I would have had men and arms to fight, not nature." The legend of Napoleon's defeat by "General Winter" was born.[8] Geoffroy did not think it necessary to douse the flames in Moscow; instead, in his 1836 tract *Napoléon and the Conquest of the World*, he had the emperor march north toward St. Petersburg, inflict a crushing defeat on the Russian army, capture Czar Alexander I, and occupy Sweden. After resurrecting the kingdom of Poland and completing his conquest of Spain, he lands an army on the East Anglian coast north of Yarmouth and pulverizes a British army of 230,000 men led by the Duke of York at the Battle of Cambridge. England is incorporated into France and divided into twenty-two French *départements*. By 1817 he has wiped Prussia from the map, and four years later he defeats a large Muslim army in Palestine and occupies Jerusalem, destroying all the mosques in the city and taking the black stone from the ruined Dome of the Rock back to Paris.[9]

This is by no means the end of his success, for in quick succession after this, Napoleon conquers Asia, including China and Japan, destroying all the holy places of other religions, establishes hegemony over Africa, and brings America under French control, following a request to this effect by all the North and South American heads of state at a congress held in Panama in 1827. In his inaugural address as "Ruler of the World," Napoleon announces that his universal monarchy "is hereditary in my race, there will from now on to the end of time only be one nation and one power in the globe. . . . Christianity is the only religion on earth." Armed with a new title conferred by the pope, *Sa Toute-Puissance*, he even finds domestic bliss once more, since the death of his Austrian wife, married only for political reasons, allows him to remarry his beloved Joséphine.

In 1832, finally, he dies, having accomplished more than any previous statesman or general in history. Far from being a ruthless dictator, he has preserved the legislature and proved a liberal and peaceful monarch. As the linkage of the victory of France with the victory of Christianity suggests, all this is due above all to the workings of Divine Providence, and in this sense at least, Geoffroy's approach was rather old-fashioned. It also incorporated a very strong element of historical or perhaps one should say pseudohistorical inevitability: one change in the course of history, at Moscow, led inexorably to a whole, lengthy chain of events that followed on without any possibility of deviation or reversal, indeed led to the end of history itself, as announced by Napoleon in his inaugural address as Ruler of the World. Even Victor Hugo did not go this far, arguing in *Les Misérables* that Divine Providence had decreed that there was no place any more in history for a colossus like Napoleon, so that Waterloo, where the prosaic and unimaginative nature of the dull military technician Wellington had proved victorious over the genius of Napoleon, marked a sharp turning point in world history in a larger sense than simply marking the end of French military glory.[10]

Of course, as Geoffroy himself well knew, Providence had decided that Napoleon should not rule the world, and he reminds readers of the reality at various points by mentioning a scurrilous alternative history within his own alternative narrative that presented Napoleon as losing a battle at Waterloo and being exiled to St. Helena, or by having Napoleon, aboard ship in the South Atlantic after conquering Asia, espy St. Helena on the horizon, a sight that sends a shiver down his spine and makes him raise his eyes for a moment beyond his fictive existence to the reality that actually encompassed him. Readers knew that Napoleon in reality had been defeated before Moscow, and that the Russians had won in 1812 precisely because they had refused to meet the French emperor in a pitched battle. Nevertheless, for all its weaknesses, Geoffroy's work is the first recognizable full-length, speculative, alternative history, and it appeared at a time, in the mid-1830s, when the Napoleonic legend was riding high, to triumph a decade and a half later with the events that followed the 1848

Revolution, above all the coup d'état of Louis Napoleon and his assumption of the title of Emperor Napoleon III. The whimsy of Pascal or Gibbon had given way here to a serious political purpose. Geoffroy himself was the adopted son of Napoleon I, who had taken him under his wing after his own father was killed at the Battle of Austerlitz, and his own full first name was not Louis but Louis-Napoleon. Still, the book's fascination and appeal continued through the nineteenth century into the twentieth, and it was frequently reprinted as a reminder to the French of what might have been, so much so that in 1937 the writer Robert Aron countered it with a narrative in which Napoleon wins the Battle of Waterloo but decides that war and conquest are a bad thing, abdicates, and goes anyway, although voluntarily, into exile on St. Helena, showing his "inner greatness" and his "insight into necessity."[11]

Geoffroy's narrative was clearly wishful thinking on the grandest possible scale. Its methodological premise was taken up and systematized two decades later, in 1857, in a series of articles by the philosopher Charles Renouvier, later published as a book. Renouvier gave it a name, by which it has been known ever since in French and German: *Uchronie.* "The writer composes an *uchronie*, a utopia of past time. He writes history, not as it was, but as it could have been."[12] Renouvier would have been more honest had he said *should* have been. His own approach was explicitly political. He described his method by means of a diagram showing a series of stages, beginning with the initial moment at which imaginary history deviates from real history, the *point de scission* that causes the *première déviation*. But while the *trajectoire imaginaire* is a single line stretching undeviatingly into the imaginary future, the *trajectoire réelle* keeps branching off into short lines with dead ends, which can only be linked by leading them back to the main line of the imaginary. The key point is the angle at which the imaginary trajectory departs from the real, and Renouvier declares that this depends on the purposes of the writer.[13] In Renouvier's case this is to advance the cause of freedom by realizing it through an imaginary past, a case he illustrates by chronicling the history of religion since the Romans with reference to the principle of toleration.

After describing the initial situation (Roman intolerance toward Judaism, which he justifies, in a manner not untypical of mid-nineteenth-century French antisemites, by calling the Jews religious fanatics who dreamed "of ruling the world," and a comparable intolerance toward early Christianity), he launches the *première déviation* by having the emperor Marcus Aurelius mistakenly declared dead in one of his campaigns, to be replaced by the general Avidius Cassius, a supporter of the Roman Republic. Later on, jointly with Marcus Aurelius, who returns to the throne, Cassius inaugurates a program of reform that creates a free peasantry instead of a slave class and eventually, through many twists and turns, leads in the Western Empire to a state religion based on the household gods along with toleration of other religions. A fanatical Orthodox Christianity triumphs in the East, leading to the Crusades, not against Jerusalem but against Rome, whose inhabitants an army of 400,000 rabidly intolerant Eastern Crusaders aims to convert to what they think of as the true teachings of Jesus, happily failing to do so as they start fighting each other over what exactly these were. In the East, intolerance leads to political chaos and defeat by the barbarians, while the tolerant Stoicism of the Western Empire survives the declaration of independence by the Gauls, Britons, Spaniards, and others, who, unencumbered by religious strife, create a federation of independent European states. Similarly, in the East, the victorious barbarians reintroduce Christianity, but in a reformed state, without the confessional, without purgatory, without monasteries, and in general without any of the trappings of Catholicism or Orthodoxy. Science and learning flourish everywhere, and Renouvier ends with an appeal to humanity to form a league of nations with an international court. By contrasting this happy story in a series of appendices with what he saw as the inhumane and unfree depredations of Catholicism through the ages, Renouvier brought out the contrast between ideal history and real history; the latter is only in his view given meaning by the former, and indeed the book is presented as the translation of an old manuscript that a family of persecuted religious noncon-formists kept in order to remind themselves that things could be different and might easily have been better.[14]

Neither D'Israeli's brief essay, published in an obscure edition that did not even appear in England, nor Geoffroy's heady Napo-leonic fantasy, popular though it was in some quarters of the French reading public, nor Renouvier's difficult and densely ar-gued anticlerical philosophical treatise, started any kind of fash-ion for speculation on different paths history might have taken. Contributions to the genre appeared only sporadically, as with the British historian G. M. Trevelyan's essay "If Napoleon Had Won the Battle of Waterloo," written for a competition staged in 1907 by the *Westminster Gazette*. Trevelyan picked up on the speculations of Victor Hugo to suggest that if Napoleon had won the Battle of Waterloo, the British would have been forced to make peace, and economic and social conditions would have deteriorated under the leadership of the archconservative Lord Castlereagh (despite a rebellion of working people led by Lord Byron, which would have been put down and the noble poet exe-cuted). British liberals would have fled to Latin America, where a reactionary British government would have joined forces with Spain to fight to keep the Spanish colonies, while on the conti-nent, despite Napoleon's influence, the ancien régime would have continued more or less as before in its unreformed, obscurantist ways. Far from launching himself on a conquest of the world, Napoleon, confronted with a France and indeed a Europe ex-hausted by more than two decades of almost continuous warfare, would have decided enough was enough and settled down to a peaceful old age. In this scenario, Napoleon finally dies while con-templating a new war to unify Italy, a war that did not happen.[15] Trevelyan was an enthusiast for Italian unification who wrote three substantial volumes on its hero, Giuseppe Garibaldi, and was a committed liberal in politics, part of a Whig tradition that included his great-uncle Lord Macaulay, one of the most vocal advocates of the extension of voting rights in 1832. His narrative of events following a putative victory by Napoleon at Waterloo is as far removed as possible from wishful thinking; it is, rather, a negative story, illustrating how badly things might have gone and thus, by implication, how Waterloo, despite a temporary wave of political repression and economic hardship in Britain, laid the foundations for the multiple triumphs of liberalism in the nineteenth century by destroying the tyranny of the French emperor. In fact, of course, as Trevelyan knew perfectly well, none of this was very plausible, for a defeat of the forces led by the Duke of Wellington in 1815 would not necessarily have meant the end of the war; the Allies might have regrouped and fought on to eventual victory; after all, their resources far outweighed those of the exhausted French by this time. Here too, therefore, was an alternative history driven mainly by political motives and beliefs.[16]

But the function of counterfactuals as entertainment was far from dead. In 1932 the first ever collection of essays in the genre appeared, edited by Sir John Collings Squire under the title *If It Had Happened Otherwise* and including a reprint of Trevelyan's piece on Waterloo. Squire was a literary critic and poet, a somewhat blimpish figure who in the 1930s sympathized with the British Union of Fascists and was incorrigibly hostile to literary modernism. He liked to project an image of a beer-drinking, cricket-loving English gentleman, in keeping with his surname — Virginia Woolf and the Bloomsbury Group were indeed wont to refer to him and his coterie as the "squirearchy" — and many of his publications were lighthearted and humorous. *If It Had Happened Otherwise* (published in the United States as *If: Or History Rewritten*) belongs to this category of his books.[17] The contributors were for the most part literary men (there were no women among them). Many of them reversed the course of history for entertainment and effect: the popular historian Philip Guedalla had a good deal of fun imagining the role of Islam in Europe if the Moors had defeated the attempt to expel them from Spain in 1492,[18] as did Harold Nicolson in speculating on Lord Byron as king of Greece. More political was the contribution by Monsignor Ronald Knox, who painted a dire portrait of what Britain would have been like had the General Strike of 1926 been victorious; ruled by trade unions and left-wing socialists, the country would have become something like Soviet Russia, with freedom of education and expression suppressed and the state controlling everything. This was another example of the dystopian version of alternative history, as practiced by Trevelyan many years before.

However, quite a few of the contributors to Squire's volume took the opportunity to indulge in a bout of wishful thinking at its most nostalgic. G. K. Chesterton's "little literary fancy"[19] speculated about what would have happened if Don John of Austria had married Mary, Queen of Scots — or in other words, England had remained, like the author, Catholic (Britain and Europe would have progressed faster than they did); the French writer André Maurois suggested that had Louis XVI been bolder and managed to avoid the French Revolution, France would have become a constitutional monarchy like Britain; the German popular historian and biographer Emil Ludwig thought that if the liberally inclined German emperor Frederick III had not died of cancer after a few months of his reign in 1888, Germany would have become a parliamentary democracy and not remained the authoritarian state that went to war in 1914, with such disastrous consequences for itself, Europe, and the world; Sir Charles Petrie, another conservative historian close to the British Fascists (though always anti-Nazi), in a chapter reprinted from an earlier publication, considered that things would have turned out better for Britain, and especially its literary and cultural life, had Bonnie Prince Charlie succeeded in his bid to seize the throne from the Hanoverians in 1745; and Winston Churchill argued that had Lee won the Battle of Gettysburg the eventual consequence would have been a union of the English-speaking peoples, something he represented in his own person as the child of an English father and an American mother. Nostalgia and regret for a history that had taken the wrong turn permeate a good number of the essays in the volume, making them something more than a mere literary amusement; a characteristic of "what-if" versions of history that was to recur with a vengeance many decades later.

Clearly, many of these fantasies would be easy to challenge, and it would not be difficult to draw out their implications plausibly enough in an entirely different direction from the one their authors imagined events would have taken. Philip Guedalla's imagined Islamic Europe (a theme already explored, as we have seen, by Gibbon and D'Israeli) bracketed out the militant Catholicism of the French, who might well have obeyed a call from the pope for a fresh Crusade against the victorious Moors in Spain; Lord Byron would probably have had no more luck in trying to control the factional and disputatious Greeks than did their real monarch, the Wittelsbach prince who became the unfortunate King Otto; the British trade unions who staged the General Strike in 1926 were moderate pragmatists who would probably have been just as horrified at the idea of a Soviet England as Monsignor Ronald Knox was; a marriage between Mary, Queen of Scots and Don John of Austria would have done nothing to make the Scottish queen less flighty or more sensible or more capable of controlling the Protestants, and the Austrian prince would have been excluded from British political life as firmly as Philip II was when he married her namesake, Mary I of England; neither Louis XVI of France nor any of his family showed the slightest inclination to become constitutional monarchs and would have restored an absolutist regime as soon as they were able; the idea that Frederick III of Germany was a liberal has been shown by a recent biography to be a myth, and in any case he was a weak character who was putty in the hands of the ruthless and unscrupulous Bismarck; Bonnie Prince Charlie may have been a romantic figure to posterity, but he too was weak and indecisive and unlikely to have changed much if he had come to the throne; and America was already too strong and independent in the 1860s even for a victorious Confederacy to contemplate a union with England. No doubt the essays were not intended to convince, merely to entertain through speculation; but already it was clear that historians needed to be more careful than Squire's contributors were about setting plausible conditions for their imaginings if they were to carry much conviction with their readers.

Squire's volume in some ways reflected the uncertainties and anxieties of British politics in the late 1920s and early 1930s, when no political party could achieve a majority in Parliament, and politicians such as Oswald Mosley and Winston Churchill crossed easily from one party to another. As the contours of British and European politics became clearer with the rise of Nazism, such speculations died away. Counterfactual essays continued to appear on occasion, some more serious, some less so, in the following years. Arnold Toynbee's massive, multivolume *A Study of History* included a handful of attempts at speculation of this kind, picking up on Gibbon and discussing what France might have been like had Charles Martel not defeated the Moors, but also imagining the consequences of a comprehensive Viking conquest of Europe.[20] In 1953 the American author Joseph Ward Moore published a novel, *Bring the Jubilee*, set in the mid-twentieth century, when the United States of America, following Lee's victory at the Battle of Gettysburg during the American Civil War (the point from which the counterfactual narrative diverges from the real timeline of history). The victorious Confederacy has conquered South America and much of the Pacific, but the Germans have won the First World War and become a rival superpower. Slavery has been abolished but technological change has been slow, with no airplanes, no lightbulbs, no cars, no telephones. While the Confederacy flourishes, the United States has been squashed into a relatively small area of North America and has descended into poverty and racial violence. The intent here is to reverse the signs of real history in the interests of satire, rather than to posit a plausible counterfactual scenario; and the science-fictional nature of the novel is confirmed when the hero discovers how to travel back in time (unlikely, given the technological backwardness posited by the author), visits the Battle of Gettysburg, and inadvertently changes the course of the battle so that Lee loses rather than wins, thus shifting the timeline back to what we ourselves have experienced in which the North defeats the Confederacy and everything follows that followed in reality. Conveniently, the hero is now trapped in the past he has created, as the world he has come from disappears without trace.[21]

Sporadic articles, usually by specialist historians speculating in their own field of research, can be found in various journals and periodicals during the 1960s and 1970s without ever inaugurating a fashion. In 1961 the American journalist William L. Shirer, author of the massive best seller *The Rise and Fall of the Third Reich*, published his brief essay "If Hitler Had Won World War II," suggesting that the Nazis would have conquered America and inaugurated a Holocaust of American Jews. Designed to try and revive American memories of the evil of Nazism, the essay fell into a period when the trial in Jerusalem of Adolf Eichmann, the Nazi official who had been the chief administrator of the extermination of European Jews, was reawakening public memory about the real crimes of Nazism. Shirer had been a press correspondent in Germany during the 1930s and had witnessed Nazi antisemitism at first hand. Convinced from the outset that Hitler enjoyed the overwhelming support of the great mass of ordinary Germans, he did not want the history of Nazism to be forgotten in an era of Cold War friendship between West Germany and the United States.[22] In a more academic vein, in 1976 the British historian Geoffrey Parker published a more serious essay in counterfactualism with a brief study on what might have happened had the Spanish Armada succeeded in landing in England in 1588: Philip II of Spain would have conquered the country and restored Catholicism, and by harnessing the rich resources of the

English economy to his global ambitions, he might well have led the Counter-Reformation to victory in Germany and established Spanish rule over North America.[23]

Parker was to return to counterfactuals four decades later with a collection of essays and a more systematic attempt to justify speculations of this kind. His essay, and the various collections that preceded and followed it, demonstrated one feature of counterfactuals, and that was that as historical speculations they always take the form of essays, usually very brief ones. Deprived of genuine empirical material, historians soon run out of steam. Lengthier counterfactual speculations have almost always taken the form of novels. A particularly notable attempt at a counterfactual novel was made in 1975 by the Italian author Guido Morselli, whose book *Past Conditional: A Retrospective Hypothesis* mixes novelistic techniques with chronicle and history to portray a world in which the stalemate of the First World War is broken in 1916 by an Austrian force that uses a secret tunnel under the Alps to launch a surprise invasion of northern Italy and penetrate into southern France. Meanwhile, a British commando unit kidnaps the Kaiser, whose typically self-important offer to have himself exchanged for 80,000 British prisoners of war arouses such indignation in Germany that the head of the government, Reich Chancellor Bethmann Hollweg, is forced to resign, and is replaced by the liberal politician Walther Rathenau, who concludes an armistice with the Allied powers after the German army has broken through their lines on the Western Front and the German navy has destroyed the British in the North Sea. Rathenau's armistice terms, which, to everyone's surprise, make no territorial demands but propose instead the creation of a federal Europe on a socialist basis, are rejected in Germany, where he is ousted in a coup amid antisemitic demonstrations and replaced by Hindenburg. The field marshal imposes a rule of such harshness on the defeated countries that resistance movements spring up everywhere, and the trade unions across Europe bring him down by a general strike, leading to the return of Rathenau and the final creation of the European socialist confederation.[24]

Morselli makes strenuous efforts to present carefully researched details taken from the real historical events of the war, just moving them around in time a little, so that the Kapp putsch of 1920, in which a right-wing coup in Berlin was defeated by a general strike, is moved forward in time and put into the hands of Hindenburg, and the military breakthroughs on the Italian and Western fronts follow a minute description of the real state of affairs preceding them, drawn from historical documents. Yet the changed historical facts that underpin his narrative are too numerous and too arbitrary to carry conviction. The secret tunnel through the Alps is a daring enough hypothesis on its own, and it is by no means certain that it would have given the Austrians the decisive advantage Morselli describes; moreover, it is not an altered historical circumstance but pure fictional invention. And to add to it the kidnapping of the Kaiser turns the whole scenario into obvious fantasy. Walther Rathenau certainly believed in European economic unity and a centrally directed economy, but far from being a socialist, he was a businessman of considerable wealth, a liberal in politics; and the idea that he would have tried to establish a political as opposed to an economic European confederation is again stretching plausibility beyond its limits.[25] In the end, the book is neither quite counterfactual history nor pure counterfactual fiction. Above all, it is an example of wishful thinking. Morselli's counterfactual history of the war follows Renouvier not only in presenting an altered past as a retrospective utopia but even in bringing it to an end with the realization of the idea of a league of nations. The only difference is that by the time Morselli was writing, such an international organization actually existed, though not at all on the basis of socialism.[26]

The following year, in the atmosphere of cautious liberation that was beginning to spread across Spain in the wake of the death of the dictator Francisco Franco, the Catalan author Victor Alba published a book entitled *1936–1976: History of the Second Spanish Republic* in which he narrated the four decades that passed from what was in reality the final crisis of the Republic as if the Civil War had never happened. Instead of falling victim to a botched military coup that led to the outbreak of three years of hostilities between Republicans and Nationalists, the government under Casares Quiroga arrests the plotters, sends Franco and his fellow generals into premature retirement, and placates the Left by nationalizing nearly a third of the economy. The altered historical starting point depends on making Quiroga a far firmer and more decisive political leader than he actually was (in reality he hesitated too long, then resigned). Like Geoffroy, Alba interspersed his narrative with glimpses of the real course events took, all the while presenting them as acts of a disordered imagination. Real people appear in the story, including Franco himself, who is reinstated as chief of the army general staff when the Germans and Italians invade in 1940, seeing in the Republic an important ally of Republican France. Guernica is bombed by the Germans as it was in reality, the poet Lorca is murdered, and events of the Civil War are transmogrified into events of a putative conflict between Spain and the Axis powers.[27] To this example of pro-Republican wishful thinking came a riposte in the shape of *The Reds Won the War*, published by Fernando Vizcaíno Casas in 1989. While Alba took great pains to provide his book with the underpinnings of academic research, the far-right Francoist Vizcaíno presented the Republicans, polemically and without troubling greatly to examine the evidence, as Communists or their willing tools, exaggerated the numbers involved in Republican massacres of Nationalist prisoners, downplayed or ignored the atrocities committed by his own side, and defamed Republican leaders as mass murderers. By indulging in distortions of such an obvious nature, however, he undermined the plausibility of his own construction, prompting even more extreme and polemical counter-fantasies from the other side, in which Franco (for example) dies a miserable death by drowning in human excrement at the outset of the conflict.

The passions unleashed by the Civil War and the decades of authoritarian rule that followed it found expression after Franco's death in Spanish counterfactual scenarios that refought the war all over again, and with increasing bitterness.[28]

Deep political crises and divisions such as these could sometimes prompt counterfactuals of a rather desperate kind. In 1972, during the political convulsions caused by the Vietnam War, the American historian Barbara Tuchman imagined that Mao Zedong and Zho Enlai had written to President Franklin D. Roosevelt in January 1945 offering to come to the White House to discuss the war in China, and particularly the conflict between their own Communist forces and the American-backed Nationalist forces of Chiang Kai-Shek. The fictional letter, supposedly suppressed up to this point, was printed by Tuchman in the journal *Foreign Affairs* and followed up by an essay on what might have happened had the offer been taken up: the United States might have been persuaded not to back the Nationalists, Mao could possibly have agreed not to regard the United States as his enemy, "there might have been no Korean War with all its evil consequences. . . . We might not have come to Vietnam."[29] But the opportunity had been lost, she hypothesized, by the obstructive behavior of the then American ambassador in China. Whether this scenario was realistic was doubtful in the end, however, not least because the American hostility to Communism was already so deep that an alliance with Mao against Chiang seemed unlikely in the extreme.

In Britain, the situation was very different. Squire's rather frivolous collection held the field for a long time. No doubt it was the essays in *If It Had Happened Otherwise* that E. H. Carr had in mind when he dismissed such speculations as a mere parlor game.[30] An attempt to get beyond this limitation was made in 1979 by Daniel Snowman, a popular historian, author, and BBC broadcaster with a long list of solid historical publications to his credit. The date of publication suggests deeper political roots in the climate of uncertainty and self-examination that prevailed in the 1970s, as the "decline of Britain" debate raged in the UK. Just as Margaret Thatcher was proclaiming that she could do better for Britain than the existing elites were doing, so Snowman was inviting historians to say how they could have done better than historical actors had managed in the past. In the introduction to his collection *If I Had Been . . . Ten Historical Fantasies* (London, 1979), Snowman complains that in speculative histories like Squire's, "there are no rules as to the degrees of 'ifness' permitted, and the results can be wildly fanciful as the mood dictates."[31] Enlisting ten professional historians in his aid, Snowman sought to reduce the arbitrariness so evident in a number of the contributions to Squire's collection by asking them

> to evoke a strictly authentic historical setting and to recreate as accurately as possible the situation facing the personality around whom their essay revolved. There was to be no *deus ex machina*, no invented assassination, no melodramatic intervention of the fates to give artificial wings to the imagination. Furthermore, our authors were asked to concentrate upon a genuine moment in the past and upon the decision-making that took place at the time: speculation about what might or might not have happened subsequently was to be only a secondary consideration. Thus, the "ifs" of this book occur within a framework carefully circumscribed by historical facts. All that is changed is that the central character of each piece is deemed to have decided upon a slightly different, but entirely plausible course of action from that actually adopted.[32]

Snowman's procedure introduces major constraining factors here, which limit the degree of speculation in an effective way. Finally, he asked each contributor to conclude his contribution (again, all the writers were male), by reflecting on its implications. This gives his collection a unity found in few others.

However, it still has problems. The first of these, as Snowman recognizes, is that by choosing "great men" (and they are indeed

all men) he is giving credence to the discredited idea that history
is made by great men and little or nothing else, where most historians would point to the role of more impersonal factors in addition or even in place of the impact of the individual. Of course,
as he concedes, "only a fool or an incurable romantic would attribute the fundamental movements of history almost exclusively
to its few leaders." Nevertheless, in the end, he sidesteps rather
than confronts this issue, by commenting simply that the essays
in his volume "are not meant to imply a view one way or the other
about the part played by the 'great' men of history so much as
to provide data for what will surely be a continuing debate."[33]
More interestingly, perhaps, Snowman broaches the subject of
free will and determinism, pointing out that the present is, or
at least seems to be, indeterminate, with a vast array of choices
of possible courses of action before us; only later do we begin to
identify the larger reasons why we took one choice rather than
another.[34] Here too, however, he leaves the issue unresolved, inevitably so perhaps, since the conditions under which his contributors are asked to imagine a different choice being made are
so carefully and narrowly circumscribed.

More seriously still, as Niall Ferguson has pointed out, Snowman's entire collection falls into the trap of wishful thinking.[35]
No historian, asked how he would have behaved had he been in
the shoes of a major historical person, is going to say he would
not have been able to match up to that person's acumen, brilliance, or boldness. The whole point of the exercise is that he's
going to do better; he's going to avoid the mistakes of his avatar, and succeed where his avatar failed. Thus Roger Thompson, as the Earl of Shelburne, prevents American independence;
Esmond Wright, as Benjamin Franklin, prevents American discontent of the same era from spilling over into revolution; Peter
Calvert, as Benito Juárez, saves the emperor Maximilian, foisted
on the Mexicans by the French, and brings decades of peace to
that troubled land; Maurice Pearton, as Adolphe Thiers, prevents
the Franco-Prussian War of 1870–71; Owen Dudley Edwards, as

Gladstone, solves the Irish Question; Harold Shukman, as the liberal democrat Alexander Kerensky, head of the provisional government in the months following the February Revolution of 1917 that overthrew the czar, prevents the Bolsheviks from coming to power; Louis Allen, as the Japanese military leader General Hideki Tojo, avoids bombing Pearl Harbor; Roger Morgan, as West German chancellor Konrad Adenauer, reunifies Germany following Stalin's note offering talks in 1952; Philip Windsor, as Alexander Dubček, averts the Warsaw Pact invasion that in reality overthrew his liberal-communist regime in Czechoslovakia in 1968; Harold Blakemore, as Salvador Allende, preserves his socialist-communist government in Chile in 1972–73 by averting a military coup.

The historians in Snowman's collection all do what historians should never do: they lecture the people of the past on how they should have done better. Do we really think we could have avoided the mistakes they made? Of course, it's easy to succumb to the temptation. But we should resist it. As Ian Kershaw remarks in his study of ordinary Germans' attitudes to the Nazi dictatorship: "I should like to think that had I been around at the time I would have been a convinced anti-Nazi engaged in the underground resistance fight. However, I know really that I would have been as confused and felt as helpless as most of the people I am writing about."[36] We can only imagine that we could do better than people in the past because we have the luxury of hindsight, and, crucially, because we are different people with different ideas and assumptions and different ways of making decisions. Snowman of course is aware of this problem, and therefore he insisted that the behavior of the historical personages whose identity the authors assumed had to be in line with what we know about them from the historical evidence. But this does not entirely get around the problem of getting into the skin of a long-dead historical actor, as he concedes.[37] In practice, what these historians do is to wish a personality change on their subjects: Kerensky becomes more decisive than he actually was, Stalin be-

comes more sincere in his 1952 note offering German reunification than he actually was, Allende becomes less muddled and
confused than he actually was, Tojo becomes less aggressive than
he actually was, Maximilian becomes less helpless than he actually was, Thiers becomes more insightful than he actually was.
Snowman's injunction to respect the personalities of the individuals into whose skin his contributors slip has to be disobeyed
if the sleight of hand is to work.

More important than any of these considerations, in the context of a discussion of alternative histories, however, is the fact
that the contributors, with rare exceptions, say little or nothing about the consequences of the alternative decisions they discuss. When they do, their speculations are so brief as to amount
to little more than tentative suggestions. Shelburne's avoidance of American independence has Queen Elizabeth II ruling
America two centuries later; the victory of Emperor Maximilian
of Mexico is thought most likely to have made little difference in
the long run, with a series of coups and dictatorships, although
the possibility is canvassed that there would have been no Mexi-
can Revolution in 1911 and thus the United States might not have
intervened in the First World War, which might also have been
averted if there had been no Franco-Prussian War in 1870. But
the intervening years are elided, with the consequence that none
of the possible events or developments that might have taken
place during them is taken into consideration. Ultimately, in fact,
these longer-term hypotheticals are of secondary interest to the
contributors, strictly subordinate to the main task given them,
of examining the decisions and impersonating the actors allotted
them and exploring their immediate historical context.[38] Moreover, these speculations put enormous imaginary power into
the hands of individual politicians, giving them retrospectively
the means to defy or overturn the massive historical forces with
which they were confronted.

Very different was the attempt made by Alexander Demandt,
a German specialist in the history of ancient Rome, to justify

counterfactuals in 1984. In his brief treatise *History That Never Happened*, he argued that "references to possible alternative developments reveal crucial events that could easily have turned out otherwise." The problem with this rather banal claim was that such references were not really necessary in order to reveal the events in question. Demandt's fifteen examples covered familiar topics such as the defeat of Charles Martel in 732 (a peaceful Europe marked by the early advance of scientific knowledge); the victory of the Spanish Armada in 1588 (a Catholic England, made liberal perhaps by Philip II's dismissal of the Duke of Alba and declaration of religious toleration); and the survival of the archduke Franz Ferdinand in 1914 (no First or Second World War). Demandt, therefore, was as prone to wishful thinking as any other counterfactualist. Nevertheless, he introduced a number of key questions that were to occupy students of the genre for some time to come, with his assertions that "alternatives remote from reality are unlikely," "events are predetermined to differing degrees," and "unlikely events stand alone"; or in other words, he raised the problem of how far, and in what way, the counterfactual imagination can be restricted or limited in some way. "Historical fantasy," he rightly observed, "needs to be checked against empirical plausibility. The measure of the unreal is the real." [39]

Demandt's treatise introduced a note of German seriousness into the subject, but Anglo-American frivolity soon reasserted itself with a slim volume of twenty-one essays by various authors, mostly British and American professional historians, edited in 1985 by the French history specialist John Merriman, a professor at Yale, entitled *For Want of a Horse: Choice and Chance in History* (a reference to the passage at the end of Shakespeare's *Richard III* in which the king is slain in battle because he is unable to find a horse to ride away on, thus inaugurating the new dynasty of the Tudors and bringing the Middle Ages in England to an end). Advertised on the front cover as "humorous speculations," the collection included brief discussions of a variety of topics, including the role of the pigeon in France, or borscht, beetroot soup, in Russia, or, more generally, bad luck (as in the case of the Stuarts, who had more than their fair share of it), or chance and contingency, as in the wrong turn taken by Archduke Franz Ferdinand's car at Sarajevo in 1914, resulting in his assassination. In fact, only five of the essays are really speculative, in the sense that they are devoted mainly to discussing alternative courses taken by events, rather than narrating the events themselves and underlining the role of chance and contingency in the way they turned out.

There are entertaining essays on what might have happened had Fidel Castro, a talented baseball player in his youth, accepted the contract that might have been offered him by the New York Giants (no Cuban Revolution); or Voltaire settled in Pennsylvania (he would have supplied ideas to the American Revolution); or the Native American girl Pocahontas not rescued the pioneer John Smith (Virginia would have failed, so no American Revolution and no Civil War); or the Confederacy won that Civil War ("Southern civility" is imposed on the Union); or James II triumphed in 1688 (England would have become Catholic again); or Governor Hutchinson managed to avert the Boston Tea Party (America would have become "another Canada"). The point of all this, however, as the editor says, is to reintroduce "playfulness and good humor" to historical writing, and not much more.[40] The derivation of large consequences from tiny events is part of the fun. Once more, in many cases, almost superhuman powers are ascribed to individual actors: do we really think James II of England had the power to turn the Protestants of England, the overwhelming majority of the population, into Catholics? And personality changes are required too. Do we really think that Fidel Castro would have forgotten his politics if he had become a professional baseball player?[41]

Frivolity and whimsicality are two of the main reasons why alternative histories have not been taken seriously by historians, even by some of those who have advanced them. Historians have always considered it their first task to find out what did happen, not to imagine what might have happened, and while the former task poses challenges of varying severity, the latter is on the face of it quite impossible, for history depends crucially on rules of evidence, and in the latter case there is little or no evidence to which those rules can be applied. Historians have traditionally been suspicious of speculation, so their reaction to "what-if" scenarios has generally been hostile or indifferent. Aviezer Tucker has asked sceptically: "What are historiographical counterfactuals good for, beyond an entertaining exercise of our imaginative faculties?" Tucker concedes that historians implicitly use counterfactuals when they designate a cause as *necessary*, implying that had it not occurred, then things would have turned out differently. But normally historians are not so bold as this, he says, rightly, and in any case, in calling a cause necessary rather than possible or contributory, they almost never speculate about the alternative course events might have taken had it not been operative.[42]

And the "what-if" question has often threatened, as it were, to put historians out of a job by reducing everything to a matter of chance. Some exponents of the genre indeed seem to delight in emphasizing tiny causes for huge events, in the spirit of Pascal's speculations on what might have happened had Cleopatra had a smaller nose; A. J. P. Taylor was a prime exponent of this approach, both in his explanation of the outbreak of the First World War in *War by Timetable: How the First World War Began* (London, 1969) and in his own autobiography, *A Personal History* (London, 1983). But if everything were the result of accident, then explanation would become impossible, and indeed Taylor himself adopted a firmly determinist approach in his book *The Course of German History*, published in 1946. No historian has earned more ridicule than H. A. L. Fisher, who in his history of Europe, written in the early 1930s, concluded despairingly that there could be "only one safe rule for the historian: that he should recognize in the development of human destinies the play of the contingent and the unforeseen" and admit that "there can be no generalizations."[43] Fisher's views have been widely rejected by historians because generalization and explanation have been seen by most of them as their principal business. If historians don't explain things, they descend to the level of chroniclers.

Then again, as we have already seen, the "what-if" question has often been attached to individuals, as in speculations about how things might have been different had Hitler died sooner or Lenin later than he did. Even E. H. Carr was in his last years prepared to admit that Soviet Russia might have been spared the worst ravages of Stalin's great purges had Lenin lived into the 1940s, as was quite possible until he was severely injured by an assassination attempt during the Russian Civil War. This suggestion — another example of large causes deriving from small events — betrays a naïve belief in the extra-historical powers of great or at least powerful men that Carr in his earlier days would not have countenanced. Carr's speculation about Lenin may itself of course be seen as a kind of wishful thinking of the sort he criticized so trenchantly in *What Is History?* In Carr's case, it betrayed a perhaps surprising tendency to want to rescue the historic reputation and legitimacy of the Bolshevik Revolution by suggesting that it had been perverted by Stalin, and blaming the mass violence, murder, and deliberate starvation of the 1930s in the Soviet Union on a single man rather than on the Soviet system itself.[44] By stressing the importance of individuals such as Lenin and Stalin, he was going counter to the move away from a "great men" approach to history in the second half of the twentieth century that occurred with the rise of social and then cultural history, which, well before he wrote, provided another reason why the "what-if" question aroused distrust.

For these reasons, therefore, historians have generally tended to avoid speculation about what might have happened and stuck, on the whole, to trying to establish and explain what did. As the great German historian Friedrich Meinecke noted: "In historiography, one usually refrains from giving an explicit answer to the question of what would have happened had a particular event fallen out differently, or if a certain personality had been removed from the action. Such considerations are called futile, and so they are."[45] But in the last couple of decades there have been signs of a change. It has come from two directions. First, from quantitative economic or econometric history, and here in particular from the American Robert Fogel, whose first major publication posited what he called a "counterfactual" assumption, that is, he built a statistical model of what would have happened to the economy of the United States if the railways had not been constructed, as a "counterfactual" hypothesis, in order to show statistically what the contribution of railways was to American economic growth, or, in other words, what difference they actually made to the American economy. This was a statistical exercise, it was not actually an attempt to imagine an America without railways, or to indulge in nostalgia about the American West in the years before the iron horse crossed the Great Plains, or to say that there had been any possibility at all, however remote, that the railways might not have been built. It had nothing to do at all with what might have been. The concept of a "counterfactual" here was precisely what it said, namely, deploying an element of what did not happen in order better to explain the consequences of what did. The power of this mode of analysis derived precisely indeed from the impossibility of imagining the counterfactual ever having had a chance of becoming, as it were, factual.[46]

Fogel's analysis was essentially statistical: the railways appeared, or rather disappeared, as an element in a series of equations, which produced roughly the same result as they did when the railways were put in; in other words, he showed that railways didn't make all that much difference to U.S. economic growth. Similar methods have been used in other areas of economic or econometric history, though they have been criticized for placing on fragile nineteenth-century statistics a weight of sophisticated number-crunching that they simply cannot bear, and for making a series of unproven and perhaps unprovable assumptions about the ways in which railway building was, or was not, linked to other parts of the economy, assumptions that in the end all went to prove the case that was being made. Finally, whatever its merits or demerits, the econometricians' use of counterfactuals had nothing to do with chance and contingency in history, rather the contrary.[47] This is not really a "what-if" question at all, since no real alternative to what happened is being posited.

Up to the 1990s, then, "what-if?" speculations on history remained essentially at the level of entertainment, appeared intermittently, and did not demand to be taken particularly seriously. At this point, however, a change came from a second direction. A spate of new collections appeared, and the flow of publications has not dried up. In 1997 Niall Ferguson edited a collection under the title *Virtual History: Alternatives and Counterfactuals* (London, 1997). This collection both expressed and boosted a renewed interest in the genre. It came out almost simultaneously with a very extensive collection of essays by American historians, *If the Allies Had Fallen: Sixty Alternate Scenarios of World War II* (ed. Dennis E. Showalter and Harold C. Deutsch, New York, 1997). 1998 saw a special issue of *Military History Quarterly* devoted to the topic, republished the following year as *What If? The World's Foremost Military Historians Imagine What Might Have Been* (New York, 1999), edited by Robert Cowley, an American military historian and founder-editor of the *Military History Quarterly*. The words "the world's foremost" were dropped from subsequent editions, but undeterred, Cowley followed this up with two more collections: *More What If? Eminent Historians Imagine What Might Have Been* (New York, 2001), and *What If? America: Eminent Historians Imagine What Might Have Been* (New York, 2005). In 2004, Andrew Roberts produced a collection entitled *What Might Have Been: Leading Historians on Twelve "What Ifs" of History* (London, 2004). Two years later, the trio of Richard Ned Lebow, Geoffrey Parker, and Philip Tetlock published *Unmaking the West: "What-If?" Scenarios That Rewrite World History* (Ann Arbor, Michigan, 2006). On both sides of the Atlantic, therefore, counterfactual history was clearly coming into fashion toward the end of the twentieth century and at the start of the twenty-first.

The vogue has continued up to the present. The year 2006 also saw Duncan Brack's collection *President Gore . . . and Other Things That Never Happened* (London, 2006), a follow-up to *Prime Minister Portillo . . . and Other Things That Never Happened* (London, 2004), and a prequel to *Prime Minister Boris . . . and Other Things That Never Happened* (London, 2011), both edited jointly by Duncan Brack and Iain Dale, the last book straying from the genre of alternative history into the even riskier field of future prediction. The most prolific of all authors in the genre, retired Greek-American military man Peter Tsouras, has published half a dozen "alternate histories," beginning in 1994 with *Disaster at D-Day: The Germans Defeat the Allies* (New York, 1994) and continuing with books on Stalingrad, the Cold War, the War in the East, the Battle of Gettysburg, and a collection of essays entitled *Third Reich Victorious: Alternate Decisions of World War II* (New York, 2002). The popular historian Dominic Sandbrook contributed a string of articles in the *New Statesman* in 2010–11 exploring similar alternative histories from British history. Jeremy Black wrote a whole book devoted to the subject of *What If? Counterfactualism and the Problem of History* (London, 2008). Doubtless there have been more contributions to the genre besides these; doubtless there will be more to come, above all in the Anglo-American intellectual world.[48]

How do we account for this recent fashion for counterfactual history? In his illuminating book *The War Hitler Never Won*,[49] Gavriel Rosenfeld ascribes it first of all to the decline and fall of the ideologies that dominated Western thought in the nineteenth and twentieth centuries. As fascism, communism, socialism, Marxism, and other doctrines vanished from the scene or were transmuted into milder, less rigid ideologies—as someone once put it, when the *isms* all became *wasms*—so teleologies vanished and history became open-ended, freeing up a space for speculation about the course or courses it might have taken.

There is a parallel here, maybe, with the end of providentialist history that enabled writers like D'Israeli, Geoffroy, and Renouvier to start thinking about alternative history in the nineteenth century. At the end of the twentieth, along with the ideologies, the concept of progress also took a hard knock, removing certainty or even probability from the future. In place of the optimism of the sixties generation came a new uncertainty, as threats like global warming, terrorism, pandemics, fundamentalist religion, and much more besides, came to create a widespread sense of disorientation and anxiety. The growing disbelief in a knowable future encouraged speculation about the course history might have taken in the past, when it too seemed to be open-ended. At the same time, the reading and cinema-going public turned to fantasy, filling the void created by the decline of the great ideologies.

Along with these general cultural changes came the emergence of postmodernism, with its scepticism about the possibility of real historical knowledge, its blurring of the boundaries between past and present, fact and fiction, and its questioning of linear concepts of time. Postmodernism restored a belief in the subjectivity of the historian as it undermined the scientific search for objectivity so characteristic of the historians of the 1970s. The British historian Tristram Hunt, writing in 2004, complained that as rigorous social history gave way to empathetic cultural history, "what we are offered in the postmodern world of contingency and irony is a series of biographical discourses in which one narrative is as valid as another. One history is as good as another and with it the blurring of factual, counter-factual and fiction. All history is 'what if' history."[50] Though Hunt was exaggerating for effect, he had a point. The digital revolution has enabled us to manipulate at will the photographic record of the past and create movies where most of what we see is computer-generated rather than a representation of reality, while cyberspace has introduced us to an alternate reality where the people we encounter are not necessarily who they seem to be. Many people now learn about medieval Europe primarily from fantastical representations such as *Game of Thrones* or *The Lord of the Rings*. On television, history is presented as infotainment, where drama-documentaries "based on a true story" appear far more frequently than less watchable attempts to represent history without fictional embellishment.[51] War games and computer simulations allow us to replay events or scenarios from the past and bring about different outcomes from the ones that happened.

Clearly some of this can be categorized as entertainment, but equally clearly, there is a new potential here for a more serious development of counterfactual history. Yet very often, such histories, as we have already seen, can slither down the slippery slope into mere wishful thinking. E. H. Carr indeed thought that counterfactualists were mostly engaged in "settling old scores; indulging fantasies; . . . and above all, titillating those quintessentially counterfactual emotions of regret (over better worlds that almost were) and relief (over worse fates that we barely escaped)." Such a charge could easily here be leveled against Carr himself in his own regret at Lenin's early death.[52] In his view, the future still belonged to a Soviet-style planned economy, and Stalin had made the process of achieving it more difficult through his crimes. Counterfactuals about the past almost always have political implications for the present. These may be of various kinds. Gavriel Rosenfeld has argued that "fantasy scenarios . . . tend to be liberal, for by imagining a better alternate past, they see the present as wanting, and thus implicitly support changing it."[53] Yet in a place and time where liberalism or socialism or some other variety of nonconservative political doctrine, government, or system dominates, it will be conservatives who want to change it, as became clear in the United States during the presidency of Bill Clinton and in the UK under the premiership of Tony Blair.

CHAPTER 2 *Virtual History*

M any times more books and essays on what their authors, following Niall Ferguson's lead in his 1997 edited volume *Virtual History*, now call counterfactual history, have appeared since 1990 than in the whole of real history before then. Counterfactual histories have now become so frequent that they need investigating as a genre in themselves. They no longer take the form of parlor games or jeux d'esprit; on the contrary, they take themselves very seriously indeed. In these collections the concept of the counterfactual is quite different from the concept employed by econometricians such as Fogel. These historians are not engaged in a notional statistical calculation, they are trying to put forward a series of serious arguments about possible, real alternatives to what actually happened.

What makes them think that what they are doing is more serious than the parlor games played by some of their predecessors or the wishful thinking indulged in by others? Their answer is that their declared purpose is to restore free will and contingency to history and to reenthrone the individual actor in a history too often studied in terms of impersonal forces. "History involving great people or pivotal events," complains Robert Cowley in the Introduction to *More What If?*, "is out of fashion. Broad trends, those waves that swell, break, and recede, are everything these days. We are left with the impression that history is inevitable, that what happened could not have happened any other way, and that drama and contingency have no place in the general scheme of human existence."[1] Similarly Jeremy Black argues that the purpose of counterfactual history is to emphasize "the contingent, undetermined character of historical change and to undermine any sense of the inevitability of the actual historical outcome."[2] "Of course this line of thought," Andrew Roberts declares in advocating the use of counterfactuals, "infuriates the Whigs, Marxists and Determinists and anyone who believes that some kind of preordained Destiny or Fate or Providence determines human existence."[3] Both Black and Roberts urge historians to liberate themselves from the tyranny of hindsight and to try and see the past as the people who lived in it saw it, full of open and undetermined possible futures. "By engaging in counterfactual thought experiments," argues Benjamin Wurgaft in a recent article, "intellectual historians could restore an awareness of sheer contingency to the stories we tell about the major texts and debates of intellectual history"[4]

Similarly, Geoffrey Parker and Philip Tetlock, in their edited collection *Unmaking the West*, denounce the presence among historians of a "bias toward retrospective determinism" and declare that "shattering hindsight complacency is the best way to make us appreciate how uncertain everything seemed before everyone became contaminated by outcome knowledge."[5] Simon Kaye, in a recent article arguing for the usefulness of counterfactuals, has declared that their main purpose is to counter "an unfortunate contemporary mindset of assumed deterministic certainty"; by underlining "the importance of human agency" in history.[6] None of this was particularly new: all previous essays in the genre have emphasized chance and contingency in history; in 1982 John Merriman, for example, declared that "chance has not always received its due from historians seeking to explain the flow of world events"; and he argued that "an appreciation of chance helps rescue professional historians from the self-indulgent temptation to try to explain everything."[7] What was new about the counterfactual history of the 1990s and 2000s was the frequency and vehemence with which a belief in chance was asserted.

Not surprisingly, most of the historians writing counterfactual history along these lines have been both politically and methodologically conservative. To a degree, they even form something of a group: John Adamson, for example, contributed both to Ferguson's collection and to Roberts's; Roberts himself contributed to Ferguson's book and to Cowley's *More What If?* as well as his own; Geoffrey Parker wrote for Cowley in *What If?* and *More What If?* as well as for his own book; while Cowley himself contributed to Roberts's volume. As Jeremy Black says, since counterfactualism gives importance to "agency—the actions usually of a small number of individuals," it is clearly more favored by right-wing historians because, he suggests, "the latter are much more prepared to embrace the concepts of individualism and free will" than left-wing historians are.[8] There are indeed few, if any, counterfactuals written from a left-wing point of view. Whatever the eddies and countercurrents along the way, the Left has generally believed that the tides of history flow in its favor. Why should left-wing historians regret what did not happen in the past when the future is still theirs? E. H. Carr's own speculations about what might have happened had Lenin lived into a ripe old age is one of the exceptions to this general rule; socialist speculations on how Hitler might not have come to power in 1933 if the Left had formed a united front in opposition to him would be another; G. M. Trevelyan's thoughts on what might have happened had Napoleon won the Battle of Waterloo a third. But in general, left-wing speculations of this kind are few and far between. Moreover, there are political and methodological reasons for the relative absence of left-wing versions of the counterfactual genre. As Tristram Hunt has pointed out,

"what if" history poses just as insidious a threat to present politics as it does to a fuller understanding of the past. It is no surprise that progressives rarely involve themselves, since implicit in it is the contention that social structures and economic conditions do not matter. Man is, we are told, a creature free of almost all historical constraints, able to make decisions on his own volition. According to Andrew Roberts, we should understand that "in human affairs anything is possible." What this means is there is both little to learn from the potentialities of history, and there is no need to address injustices because of their marginal influence on events. And without wishing to be over-determinist, it is not hard to predict the political intention of such a reactionary and historically redundant approach to the past.[9]

In practice, therefore, counterfactuals have been more or less a monopoly of the Right.

The counterfactualists routinely stress their belief in contingency and chance as a corollary of their championing of the rights of the individual. There may, however, be more to this than meets the eye. E. H. Carr thought that "in a group or a nation which is riding in the trough, not on the crest, of historical events, theories that stress the role of chance or accident in history will be found to prevail."[10] The same might be said a fortiori of imaginative constructions of what might have been, grounded as so many of them are in a sense of regret at what actually is. It may be, indeed, that British historians of a conservative inclination began to emphasize the role of chance and think about how things might — perhaps, should — have turned out differently in the mid-1990s, because a long period of Conservative Party dominance, beginning in 1979, was clearly coming to an end, with the replacement of Conservative heroine Margaret Thatcher by the colorless John Major, whose policies were increasingly disputed by a new generation on the Tory right, to which the counterfactualists clearly belonged, and whose government, weakened and divided by faction, was replaced by Tony Blair's New Labour administration in 1997.

The principal target of the counterfactualists was clearly Marxism, or what they imagined to be Marxism. Naming three leading Marxist historians, Andrew Roberts, for example, declares that "anything that has been condemned by Carr, Thompson *and* Hobsbawm must have something to recommend it."[11] Carr in fact did not really belong in this short list. From Carr's point of view, formed during his early career, when he was a Foreign Office

mandarin, history that emphasized the role of chance or speculated on what might have been was useless because it could not
form the basis for policy, which is why he dismissed the history of
defeated alternatives to what actually happened as not worth pursuing (he was not a Marxist or even a socialist historian, as some,
including Niall Ferguson, have wrongly claimed; he was in his
own work not really interested in causes at all, only outcomes).[12]
This was a dangerous doctrine, however, that reduced historical
investigation to the status of an adjunct to present-day politics,
and it did not recommend itself to most historians, least of all at
a time, in the 1960s, when the new social history was uncovering
and celebrating the forgotten and downtrodden in the past, from
Eric Hobsbawm's studies of peasant millenarians and social ban-
dits in the Mediterranean world to Edward Thompson's resolve
"to rescue the poor stockinger, the Luddite cropper, the 'obsolete'
hand-loom weaver, the 'utopian' artisan, and even the deluded
follower of Joanna Southcott, from the enormous condescension
of posterity."[13] Carr's disdain for what he regarded as failures in
history caused him to lump together investigations of history's
victims and losers with speculations about history's missed alternatives and frustrated developments in a single pot.

Although Carr was never really a Marxist, genuine Marxist
historians such as Hobsbawm and Thompson were firmly in the
counterfactualists' firing line. This was all the more striking in
view of the fact that Marxism was fast disappearing from the
intellectual scene when they were writing, following the fall of
the Berlin Wall in 1989. In a sense the counterfactualists were
flogging an ideological dead horse, or perhaps shooting a straw
man by criticizing something that none of these historians, nor
indeed any Marxist not shackled to the dogmas of Stalinism,
had ever actually said. The idea that history should be open to
notions of contingency and chance was not news to Hobsbawm
or Thompson, and even Carr's *History of Soviet Russia* gives over
considerable space to the personalities and policies of individuals such as Trotsky, Bukharin, and Zinoviev in the aftermath of

Lenin's death.[14] Real, dogmatic insistence on historical inevitability at every stage can only be found in political texts like Stalin's *Short Course* history of Soviet Communism, not in practicing Marxist historians; and even Stalin and his followers ended up, of course, by insisting on the relative autonomy of the "superstructure," or in other words, the freedom of Communist leaders like Lenin and himself to override broader historical processes and structures, for example, pushing the Russian Revolution on from a "bourgeois revolution" in February 1917 — a revolution that Marxist theory suggested should lead to a liberal-capitalist regime lasting decades — to a "socialist revolution" within a few months.

Ignoring such easy targets, Ferguson in particular directed his fire at Marx and Engels themselves, above all for their contempt for "free will," which he says they expressed in statements such as "Men make their own history but they do not know that they are making it," or in the question posed by Marx: "Are men free to choose this or that form of society for themselves?" leading to the answer "By no means."[15] Yet Marx himself did not treat human beings as helpless in the face of big historical forces in the way that these carefully selected quotations suggest. In a famous statement *not* quoted by Ferguson, he declared that "People make their own history, but they do not make it just as they please; they do not make it under circumstances chosen by themselves, but under circumstances directly found to be already there, given and transmitted from the past."[16] Moreover, Marx never intended his general theory to explain specific events (although he did not always stick to this in practice, least of all in his journalism), rather, he meant it as an aid to understanding general trends. Ultimately, the argument here is not about history at all but about free will. As Allan Megill says, all historians assume "that human beings are both determined and free, both subordinate to external forces and capable of creating and exploiting such forces." Ferguson, Roberts, and their fellow counterfactualists are basing their arguments on an unrealistic polarization of total freedom of will on the one hand, and complete subservience to impersonal historical forces on the other, which very few historians, or indeed very few people in their own daily lives, would in practice endorse: most human action takes place between these two imaginary poles. So the bold declarations by Roberts, Black, Cowley, and others are beside the point; each case has to be decided on its own merits by historical investigation.[17]

It was not merely Marx and Engels who emphasized the constraining influence on human affairs of factors beyond human control. The great French historian Fernand Braudel, in his epic history of *The Mediterranean and the Mediterranean World in the Age of Philip II*, posited three levels of history, using the sea as a metaphor: the deep, unchanging, still waters of the environment that framed peasant life in a preindustrial age; the slow-moving waves of economic and social change; and the froth and foam of political history on the surface. Braudel went much further than Marx in reducing the room for maneuver of individual human beings, perhaps reflecting his own predicament as he wrote the first draft of his book in a German prisoner-of-war camp in the early 1940s. For him, the overwhelming majority of people in the early modern period, living on the land and subsisting from its produce, were mere insects, helpless in the face of larger forces. Braudel did not satisfactorily link his different levels of history to one another and so never developed a convincing approach to questions of historical causation. He was unable to show how political history was shaped by larger factors, except in rather minor ways like the time it took to get a letter from Milan to Madrid in the sixteenth century. His political history operated more or less independently from his social, economic, and environmental history and did indeed, as the last sections of his great study showed in what was a relatively conventional narrative of political events, have a good deal of room for maneuver in making decisions, fighting battles on land and at sea, or engaging in faction fighting at court; the point his book as a whole was trying to make was that all of this political activity made little difference to the lives of ordinary working people on the land (a demonstrably flawed assertion, as peasants quickly discovered when marauding armies marched across their fields, devastating the crops and spreading epidemics).[18]

So Braudel was not really a determinist in the sense of reducing political events to epiphenomena of larger historical forces. Indeed, when it came to narrating political history, he was as enthusiastic about counterfactuals as anyone else: "It may be a bad habit to rewrite history as it never was," he once said, "to alter the course of major events so as to imagine what might have happened. But although a sleight-of-hand like this may be an illusion, it is not pointless. In its own way, it measures the weight of events, episodes and actors, who were believed, or believed themselves, to be responsible for the entire course of history." Among other things, Braudel imagined a France in which Protestantism had become the dominant religion without any major conflict by being imposed on the country by Francis I, contemporary of Henry VIII of England.[19]

Nevertheless, Niall Ferguson, in the introduction to his *Virtual History* collection, declares that his collection of counterfactual essays is a "necessary antidote" to historical determinism such as that which he accuses Braudel of practicing and Marx of preaching.[20] What is determinism, and how can counterfactuals undermine it? In its normal dictionary sense "determinism" means the belief that events are, or can be, caused by forces external to the human will, that is, that things don't only happen because people want them to happen, they can also happen as a result of factors beyond their control. Put in this way, determinism would seem to be a doctrine that few historians in practice could object to; you can't always get what you want, as the Rolling Stones remind us, and what you get might not be the result of what someone else wants either; long ago, Sir Herbert Butterfield pointed out that the titanic religious struggles of the Reformation and post-Reformation period between Catholics and Protestants ended in an outcome that neither of them wanted, namely, the emergence of religious toleration and Enlightenment scepticism.[21]

This all seems unexceptionable enough. But what Ferguson appears to mean by determinism is not the idea that human will is circumscribed by impersonal forces, but a number of other things, which it is important to disentangle. Indeed, as Aviezer Tucker has pointed out, for Ferguson, determinism is "a conceptual blanket that covers several otherwise independent historiographical doctrines and methods of which he disapproves."[22] It is important, therefore, to look at these in turn. There are four main concepts covered by the label of determinism in Ferguson's justification of counterfactuals. *First*, there is teleology, the writing of history in terms of how it moved toward a given end. Whig historians like Trevelyan saw the whole of British history, and by implication the history of all other nations as well, as leading up to the establishment of liberal democracy; Marx saw history as leading up to the creation of a socialist society. Viewed on a global scale, both of these teleologies rearranged past events and developments along a straight line leading to a predicted but as yet unrealized future. Tucker argues that the claim that history is predetermined in this way cannot be tested by evidence since we don't and can't know the future. A counterfactual might be used to cast doubt on a teleology at some point along its trajectory, but it can't undermine it as a whole because we don't know where that trajectory will end. It follows therefore that counterfactuals can only cast doubt on teleological theories of history at a metaphysical level; a counterfactual scenario positing some possible alternative course taken by events in the short or medium term can always be got around by anyone determined enough to assert the validity of a teleology in the long term.

Second, by determinism Ferguson means the idea that political events are determined by social and economic forces.[23] This, of course, is something that Marx and Engels never said; all they said was that the broad long-term development of history from one social formation to another was relatively unaffected by individuals and discrete political and military events. They were not, in other words, saying anything about the immediate causes of specific historical happenings. Nevertheless, these can obviously get in the way of the broader trends whose overriding importance they were so insistent on emphasizing. Ferguson goes on to note how later Marxists, beginning with the early Russian theorist Georgii Plekhanov, attempted to reconcile obvious contingent factors such as military victories in battles that might easily have gone the other way, or the chance that one or other historical figure, like Robespierre or the first Bonaparte, might have died prematurely, before making his mark, with the Marxist insistence on the ultimate inevitability of political changes consequent on changes in the mode and forces of production, by declaring that individuals might influence how things happened, when and where, but not the general trend of history, which was determined by broader factors, namely, changes in the relations of production. Counterfactual speculations, Ferguson suggests, can undermine such arguments by positing alternative courses of history that are completely detached from social and economic forces. Yet this argument carries with it the danger of reducing everything to chance and eliminating all consideration of longer-term causes of major historical events.

In trying to answer the question of why Hitler came to power, for example, Ferguson complains that German historians "remain deeply committed to the idea that 'the German catastrophe' had deep roots."[24] Is he really saying it was all a matter of chance? A more fruitful way of approaching it, surely, would be to follow the lead taken by Plekhanov and say that factors such as the structure of German society, the nature of German political culture since Bismarck, the weaknesses of the Weimar Republic, the disastrous performance of the German economy in the 1920s and early 1930s, the humiliations imposed on Germany by the victorious Allies in the Peace Settlement of 1919, and other, similar factors, clearly help explain why democracy failed, but they do not explain precisely the timing or the nature of Nazism's triumph or indeed lead to the claim that the Nazis and not, say, a different form of dictatorial regime with the German military in charge and the Nazis only lending support would have come to power in 1933. For this one has to adduce further, personal factors such as Hitler's refusal to enter any coalition government except as its head, the machinations of the clique gathered around President Hindenburg, and so on. Adducing these longer-term causes does not commit one to the view that Hitler's seizure of power was inevitable, but it does suggest strongly that Weimar democracy was doomed by the early 1930s. It does not require a counterfactual to establish the role of contingency in these events, simply an examination of the evidence. What is crucial for the historian is working out how chance and contingency operate in a context that constrains the extent to which they can have an impact.

Many counterfactualists take as their starting point familiar chance events that we already know occurred: the flight of Louis XVI and Marie-Antoinette from Paris that was intercepted at the town of Varennes, resulting in their capture and eventual execution by the revolutionaries; or the failure of the Gunpowder Plot to blow up the English king and Parliament in 1605; or the wrong turn taken by Archduke Franz Ferdinand's driver in Sarajevo in 1914 that brought him into the path of the assassin; or the ill winds that scattered the Spanish Armada in 1588. Often, their speculations center on the chance survival of assassination attempts, the untimely deaths of kings, the unfortunate mortality of their offspring, the sudden reversal of fortunes in battles. Few historians would deny that such chance events had a major effect; yet for serious consequences to ensue, most historians would agree that other, larger factors had to come into play, of whatever kind. It would be easily possible to argue for instance that had Louis XVI escaped to head up an Austrian-led army in trying to suppress the revolution, the determination of the revolutionaries to protect their achievements would only have been redoubled; that the death of the political elite in England in 1605 would have radicalized English Protestants, who would have exterminated the Catholics in a bloodbath of biblical proportions; that the Bosnian Serb terrorists who failed to kill Franz Ferdinand in June 1914 would have tried again until they succeeded, with similarly cataclysmic results; or that a Spanish army landing in England in 1588 would have met with a crushing defeat by Elizabeth I and her armies and other supporters, so popular had she become by that time. Any of these events could easily have ended otherwise than it did, but larger changes in the historical context would probably have been necessary for this to have had the effects sometimes claimed by counterfactualists. Counterfactuals such as these can only be posited as having big effects by leaving out the historical context; though bringing it in does not mean the larger scheme of things would have been the same had the small event gone differently, it does reduce the scale of the change.

These examples have already taken us a long way from social and economic forces. The real question at issue here, however, is not the nature of the larger historical forces concerned, but how one prioritizes them. This brings us to the *third* type of determinism allegedly vulnerable to attack from counterfactuals, namely, the idea that history is determined by general laws of development such as those laid down for example by Arnold Toynbee in his *Study of History*.[25] The debate on laws in history goes back a long way, but at no point have historians actually accepted that history is governed by laws operating in the sense of scientific laws; history is never rigidly predictable in the way that, say, chemical reactions are. We might emphasize some kinds of causal influences over others, or deploy a theory, say, a variant of Marxism or modernization theory, to help explain the past, but saying that some factors in history depend on others — say, cultural developments are dependent on social developments, or military strength is dependent on economic strength — does not commit us to a belief in predictability. And if we say that some factors are dependent on others, we are also saying that some are more independent than others. "Accident is relative to a system, not indeterminist."[26] Historians never operationalize theory in a rigid or undeviating way; the messiness of the past and the evidence it has left behind do not allow this. As Plekhanov suggested, Marxist historians commonly use "coincidental intervening variables and auxiliary theories to explain away the obvious deviation of history from what their favored theory would lead us to expect."[27] In Tucker's words, "historiographical counterfactuals as such are not a challenge to privileging theories as such." If determinism means that there are laws of historical development, then, according to Tucker, it is not clear "how counterfactuals can do a better job of refuting these theories than plain historical facts."[28]

Fourth, following Hayden White, Ferguson argues that writing history as narrative trope — presenting a historical sequence as tragic or comic, for example — is necessarily deterministic because it presumes a specific outcome by virtue of historical style rather than historical content. Yet in my view it is not necessarily deterministic at all, because the trope does not precede the narrative but follows it. In other words, we put together a narrative then decide whether it is tragic or comic according to what seems fitting. Nor does this in any way commit the narrator to a particular view of discrete events or personalities; rather, it is a judgment on them, reached at the end of the presentation of the narrative. Hayden White, of course, argued that the framing of a narrative in one of these modes predetermined the selection of the constituent elements of the narrative. Any history beyond mere chronicle or antiquarianism was in his view a *metahistory* expressing a particular narrative trope created by the historian and not testable by empirical research. But of course, any practicing historian will tell you that this is not the case; we may devise an interpretative hypothesis but we are constantly revising it by examining the evidence for and against it, and our end product is likely to come up with something rather different than what we started out with.[29]

White's claim that all history can be allocated to one or other of a small number of narrative tropes may hold good for the classic Victorian epics he studied like Macaulay's *History of England*, but it does not apply to modern analytical history, which he does not discuss at all. And in practice there is always evidence that will not fit comfortably into a tragic or comic story, which we cannot ignore or explain away. Most historians who have told the life story of Mary, Queen of Scots, for example, have seen it as a tragedy with Mary as the victim of Tudor power politics: Mary was brought up in sixteenth-century France, expelled from Scotland as a Catholic by grim and censorious Protestants after a turbulent private and political life on the throne, imprisoned by Queen Elizabeth I of England as a threat to her position and that of the Protestant Reformation because she was next in line to the English throne, and finally executed after being implicated in a series of plots to seize the throne for herself. But nobody has sought to deny that she was herself in part to blame for her travails and her eventual death, and any historian who for instance simply failed to mention her involvement in the Babington Plot or the Throckmorton Plot, both of which aimed with Mary's approval to kill Elizabeth and seize the throne, would not be taken seriously.

In practice, therefore, choosing a particular narrative mode is only a broad moral judgment, it does not impose any specific interpretation or moral judgment on the particularities of the evidence, and it does not deny the operation of contingency (for example, the exposure of Throckmorton when he was observed by the queen's agents visiting the French embassy with suspicious frequency). In the end, too, White concedes that it is possible to ascertain the factuality or otherwise of particular events in history through the use of evidence (a concession he was forced to make when it was pointed out to him that scepticism on this point opened the door to Holocaust denial). Thus—as every practicing historian knows—factual evidence plays a significant role on its own account in shaping a narrative; we cannot simply select the facts that suit our narrative and ignore the ones that don't. What Ferguson calls "narrative determinism" doesn't therefore imply an arbitrary process of constructing a form of historical inevitability, nor, once more, is it easy to see how counterfactuals are necessary to undermine this process, since narrative by its very nature is going to mention chance events, things that might have turned out differently from the way they actually did.[30]

At times, Ferguson's attack on determinism seems to verge on an attack not only on any notion of wider forces and deeper currents in history, but on any concept of causation at all. Calling the development of chaos theory and the scientific concept of indeterminacy as his witnesses, he suggests that human affairs are becoming more subject to individual free will, not less. For Ferguson, almost any attempt to argue that a large event or process like the rise and fall of the British Empire or the outbreak of the English Civil War, has large causes, is convicted of determinism because in listing a series or hierarchy of causes, a historian like — in these two cases, respectively, Paul Kennedy and Lawrence Stone[31] — strongly implies that the event was inevitable. Ferguson makes great play with chaos theory, symbolized by the fluttering of a butterfly's wings in Japan leading to a hurricane in Bermuda — an example, incidentally, of the linkage of tiny causes to large effects so beloved of counterfactualist historians and so scorned in theory by Ferguson in his critique of Merriman's volume. Those who argue that history is essentially chaotic — that is, predominantly the produce of chance — have always had to concede that larger systems of causation still exist, determining the overall pattern of events though not their precise nature or timing. Chaos theory is not susceptible to mathematical proof in its application to history, as it is in science; in fact, it is not applicable at all. There is no measurable evidence that human affairs are becoming more chaotic, whatever may be happening in the universe out there. "Believers in chaotic history," as Tucker points out, "must assume counterfactual situations in which the initial conditions were slightly different but the outcome was radically other."[32] But this depends of course on isolating a particular cause or condition and identifying it as necessary rather than subsidiary; in other words, in order to create a counterfactual, we have to say that the condition or cause that we are altering was the decisive one, otherwise we are simply altering a rather trivial factor that most historians would agree made little difference to the outcome under consideration. This leads us back again to the very notion of a hierarchy of causes that Ferguson considers so deterministic.

Counterfactuals, then, do not do the job of undermining determinism in any of its possible meanings as well as simple factual evidence does. But this is not of course the only way in which their proponents claim that they are useful or even, in some cases, essential. They can show that particular events and decisions were not inevitable but governed by chance and contingency. By carefully scrutinizing the options confronting decision makers in an event such as, for example, the outbreak of World War I, we can come to understand better the decisions they eventually took. In doing so, says Ferguson, we should examine the possible alternatives to what happened, but of course, he adds, crucially, the number and variety of these possible alternatives is not infinite. On the contrary, it is obvious that the historian should only consider alternative outcomes that were at least plausible, or in other words, he says, possible alternatives that contemporaries themselves actually considered and wrote about (for if they did not write about them there is no evidence that they considered them). On the face of it, this seems a perfectly reasonable way of proceeding. This would, however, rule out factors such as impulsive behavior, human accident, unanticipated errors, and the like, and so reduces the role of contingency to a negligible quantity because only carefully considered and debated conditions could be taken into account.[33] Moreover, by conceding that the number of possibilities was finite, Ferguson is to my mind actually agreeing with Marx's dictum that people do not exercise their will with absolute freedom because the conditions under which they live and act are not of their own choosing and are often subject to forces beyond their control. It is after all such forces — economic, power-political, cultural, social, intellectual, geographical, or whatever—that constrain the operation of the human will, not any defects or weaknesses in the human will itself, as many a tyrant, from Napoleon to Hitler, has found to his cost. Still, the constraints are no more than constraints, and within them, decision makers were still able to choose from a number of options available to them.

Thus, for example, in July and August 1914, British foreign secretary Sir Edward Grey had the option of declaring war on Germany, or keeping Britain out of the conflict by remaining neutral; a declaration of war on, say, France or Russia was not an option in the context of the time. What can the counterfactual hypothesis of British neutrality do to help us understand why Grey did not go down that particular road? In his contribution to *Virtual History*—"The Kaiser's European Union"—and in his book *The Pity of War*, Ferguson examines this question in detail. After the war, he points out, and ever since, participants and historians have concluded that Britain's involvement in the war was inevitable, given the German violation of Belgian neutrality, which was guaranteed by the British, and the threat a German victory posed to the balance of power in Europe and, above all, Britain's empire overseas. Neutrality seemed out of the question. Yet, says Ferguson,

> The neglect of the neutrality "counterfactual" is a tribute to the persuasiveness of such emotive postwar apologies. Britain, we have come to accept, could not have "stood aside" for both moral and strategic reasons. Yet a careful scrutiny of the contemporary documents—rather than the relentlessly deterministic memoir accounts—reveals how very near Britain came to doing just that. While it seems undeniable that a continental war between Austria, Germany, Russia and France was bound to break out in 1914, there was in truth nothing inevitable about the British decision to enter that war. Only by attempting to understand what would have

happened had Britain stood aside can we be sure the right decision was made.[34]

In Ferguson's view, what would have happened in the event of neutrality shows conclusively that Grey's decision to enter the war was the wrong one. If Britain had stayed out, German war aims would have been more modest, and the Germans would have won.

Having achieved the hegemony over the rest of Europe that they had achieved by the end of the twentieth century anyway, through their creation and domination of the European Union, the Germans would not have felt frustrated and defeated, there would have been no Hitler and no Second World War, and there would have been no mass slaughter on the battlefields of Europe between 1939 and 1945, no gas chambers, no Holocaust. As Ferguson writes, "Had Britain stood aside even for a matter of weeks [in 1914], continental Europe could therefore have been transformed into something not wholly unlike the European Union we know today, but without the massive contraction in British overseas power entailed by the fighting of the two world wars."[35] The British Empire would have survived, and Britain would have continued to be a superpower throughout the twentieth century instead of declining to the level of a mere constituent part of a German-dominated united Europe.

Ferguson's counterfactual speculations, written in 1997, dovetailed with those of *Churchill: The End of Glory*, a book published by another young British conservative historian, John Charmley, five years before. Charmley broke any number of taboos with this highly critical account of Winston Churchill's leadership in the Second World War.[36] Charmley accused Churchill, after he became prime minister in 1940, a few months following the outbreak of the Second World War, of making a fatal decision by insisting on continuing to fight Hitler. In doing so, he threw away vast sums of money, leaving Britain too weak to hold on to the British Empire after the war was over. Yet this was not just bad for Britain, it was bad for the colonies too, since they would have been much better off in every way had they not achieved independence but remained under the benign and civilizing control of London. Churchill surrendered British freedom of action to the United States, who lent money and equipment to Britain on a grand scale, and used the debt to blackmail the United Kingdom into surrendering the empire — one of the chief aims of U.S. president Franklin D. Roosevelt all along. Roosevelt ran rings round Churchill at the peace summits, laying the foundations for a postwar world order dominated by America rather than Britain. The war failed to protect Poland from tyranny, first that of Hitler then that of Stalin. At home, Churchill focused obsessively on the conduct of the war, allowing the Labour Party ministers in his coalition government to convince the electorate of their fitness to govern. This enabled their victory in the 1945 election and what Charmley sees as their disastrous creation of the modern welfare state between 1945 and 1951, a development that created a culture of dependency and complacency that led to a rapid decline of Britain until Mrs. Thatcher's radical reforming Tory government began to rein back the state and create a culture of enterprise and initiative in the decade after 1979. Charmley's conclusion was devastating: Churchill, he declared, stood for the British Empire, for British independence, and for an "anti-Socialist" vision of Britain; but by July 1945 the first of these was about to fall, the second was solely dependent on America, and the third had just vanished in a Labour election victory.

How different everything would have been, claimed the maverick right-wing Tory historian and politician Alan Clark when he reviewed Charmley's book, had Churchill given way to the appeasers, led by Lord Halifax, in the spring of 1940, when they were urging a compromise peace with Germany following the catastrophic defeat at Dunkirk. Churchill foolishly rejected the "excellent terms" that Clark claimed the deputy leader of the Third Reich, Rudolf Hess, brought with him when he flew to Scotland a year later. If he had made peace with the Nazis, Clark argued, Churchill could have saved the empire by moving forces from the European theatre to the Far East to protect Malaya, Singapore, and Burma from the Japanese. With the British out of the war, the Americans would not have come in, and Hitler's Third Reich and Stalin's Soviet Union would have fought each other to a standstill on the eastern front, destroying each other in the process and weakening Russia to such an extent that it would not have been able to extend its grip on the rest of Eastern Europe after the war. Moreover, leaving the war in 1940 or even in May 1941 would not have meant abandoning the Jews of Europe to their fate, since the Nazi extermination program had not yet got under way, and in any case the British did little or nothing to rescue the Jews even when they did decide to carry on fighting the Nazis. At the same time, Charmley pointed out that in reality British governments had done nothing to prevent the mass murders and forced deportation of entire peoples in the Soviet Union during and after the war. Britain had no reason to be proud of its conduct in the Second World War, then. As both Clark and Charmley insisted, British involvement in the quarrels of continental European powers had been disastrous.[37]

These counterfactual speculations rest on an extremely shaky empirical basis. There are five main areas in which they fail to convince. *First*, as far as August 1914 is concerned, the argument that Germany was not a threat to British interests is contradicted by Ferguson himself, who in *The Pity of War* does indeed argue at one point that Germany was not powerful enough to be a serious challenge to Britain in 1914, but goes on to assert at another that the German war machine was more efficient and effective than the British because it killed more of the enemy at a lower financial cost to itself.[38] Actually, if you take the principle of calculation behind it you will find that the most efficient nations in the war were Turkey and Serbia, which spent only a tiny proportion of their national wealth on the war but succeeded in killing a very large number of their enemies all the same. The calculation, in the end, doesn't mean very much. In any case, there is no actual evidence that German war aims would have been more limited if

Britain had stayed out of the war, or, to put it another way, there is no evidence that Britain's entry into the war led to an immediate widening of German war aims beyond what they had originally been. Most of the aims of the notorious September Program of 1914 did not concern Britain anyway. What peace terms, in any case — to move on to the *second* set of empirical, evidential problems with the counterfactual of British neutrality — would Hitler have offered? In a number of speeches following the German conquest of western Europe, he made a point of holding out an olive branch to the British, but close examination of the speeches reveals them to have been entirely lacking in specificities of any kind. Actual negotiations never began, so we shall never know what conditions might have been laid down. Undoubtedly the spring of 1940 was the crucial moment, and it is entirely possible that Halifax's peace party might have come out on top, though we do not need counterfactual speculation to tell us that. As for Rudolf Hess's flight to Scotland, all the available German sources indicate that it was undertaken without Hitler's approval, and that Hitler and the other Nazi leaders were shocked and dismayed when they learned about it. He did not bring any "terms," excellent or otherwise. No convincing documentation exists of any attempt by British appeasers to invite him over.[39]

One might argue that had Britain not entered, or stayed in, either of the two wars, the German government of the day would eventually have declared war on Britain anyway, and with vastly greater chances of success had it succeeded in defeating its continental enemies in the meantime, or alternatively used a compromise peace to dismantle the British Empire bit by bit. This at least is what Churchill himself told his war cabinet on 28 May 1940:

> It is idle to think that if we tried to make peace now, we should get better terms from Germany than if we went on and fought it out. The Germans would demand our fleet — that would be called "disarmament" — our naval bases and much else. We should become a slave state though a British

government which would be Hitler's puppet would be set up — under Mosley or some such person.[40]

Churchill's views provided a better basis for counterfactual speculation than either Ferguson or Charmley was able to muster. Contrary "what-if" speculations can be proposed that are just as plausible as the ones put forward by those historians who think that Britain would have done better to have kept out of European wars and let the continentals slug it out among themselves. Take, for instance, what one might perhaps term a counter-counterfactual about the Second World War, by the left-liberal historian Paul Addison:

> The British . . . could have negotiated a peace which left Britain itself — with the possible exception of the Channel Islands — free of occupying forces. The monarchy, Big Ben and the Mother of Parliaments would have carried on as though nothing unusual had happened. But on the periphery of a Nazified Europe a vanquished Britain would gradually have become a satellite state whose domestic politics were overshadowed by the triumph of Fascism and the fear of offending Germany. Sir Oswald Mosley and his supporters would have become for the first time a force to be reckoned with, and Fascism a creed with a magnetic attraction for the rising young men of the right. How long would it have been before Hitler called for the suppression of anti-German elements in British politics? How long would it have been before he demanded British co-operation in a European programme to "resolve the Jewish problem"?[41]

This is at least as plausible as the scenario painted by Charmley and Clark.

Indeed Andrew Roberts has endorsed the view taken by Addison. He argues that a separate peace with Britain would have led to a German victory over the Soviet Union because Hitler would not have needed to deploy troops in the Mediterranean, or at least North Africa, to support Mussolini. Hitler's assurances to the British, contrary to what Charmley assumes, were patently insincere, and victory in Russia would have been followed by a full-scale invasion of the United Kingdom. In rejecting a separate peace, says Roberts, "Churchill was therefore right."[42] However, Roberts is stretching his counterfactual to breaking point and beyond, since it is extremely uncertain whether Hitler would actually have been able to defeat the Soviet Union even with Britain out of the reckoning. C. J. Sansom, author of the counterfactual novel *Dominion*, published in 2012, which takes a German-dominated Britain in the 1950s as its historical context, still thinks the war in the east was "always militarily unwinnable [for the Germans]; the country was just too vast, and the population totally hostile."[43] Contrary to what Roberts claims, the weakening of Operation Barbarossa by the deployment of German troops to rescue the failed Italians at least to the north of the Mediterranean would most likely have happened anyway, given the Italians' lamentable performance against the Greek army in 1941. The "ifs" here are too large and too numerous to be plausible, especially given the vast depth and breadth of the Soviet Union's resources. From the start of Operation Barbarossa, the Germans never committed less than two-thirds of their military resources to the Eastern Front, and a bit more would probably not have made that much difference.

Third, as far as the British Empire is concerned, nobody can prove that Britain would have kept the empire had it remained neutral in either 1914 or 1939–45. Had Germany won the First World War following a British refusal to fight, who is to say that the Kaiser and his generals would not have turned their envious eyes toward the British Empire, for which their High Seas battle fleet, under construction since Tirpitz's plan to confront and cripple or destroy the Royal Navy in the North Sea, had been launched at the end of the nineteenth century? Historians are generally agreed that Germany's longer-term foreign policy aims leading up to both 1914 and 1939 went much further than merely establishing economic hegemony over the European continent. In both cases there are clear contemporary indications that the German government was issuing a challenge, among other things, to the British Empire and British world power. Hitler's professed admiration for the empire, cited by Ferguson as an indication that he might have wanted to preserve it, was intended in reality to hold it up as an example for Germany to follow. Yet another counterfactual scenario, developed by the German-American historian Holger Herwig, has the collapse of the British Empire actually preceding a separate peace, with a German victory in the east followed by the German conquest of the British-ruled Middle East and a threatened invasion of India.[44]

In reality, of course, there is a huge amount of evidence to indicate that the continued rise of American power on the one hand, and more importantly the changing and evolving nature of society and politics in the Indian, African, and other colonies on the other, were the real forces behind decolonization in the post–Second World War era, in other words, that this was a process that no amount of money and resources saved by Britain not spending billions of pounds on the war effort could have brought to a halt. The British Empire had been in long-term decline since the Boer War, and noninvolvement in a European war, Sansom has claimed, would only have accelerated this process, not only in 1940 but also, arguably, in 1914. Parts of the Empire, such as Australia or New Zealand, would not have accepted a separate peace in 1940, he speculates, and a link with Germany would have sparked uncontrollable unrest in India (itself already on the way to Dominion status by 1939). The weakness of a subjugated Britain would have been obvious to everyone across the globe, and would probably have led to an upsurge in national independence movements, above all in South Asia.[45] Finally, the hypothesis that Britain might have been better off had the empire been retained ignores the enormous cost of running the empire in terms of manpower and resources as well as the increasingly negative impact of British rule in its later phases, from atrocities in Kenya and Malaya to famine and disease in India. Not every post-colonial state formerly ruled by the British has failed to develop or disintegrated into chaos and civil war. Moreover, it is just as arguable that the liberation of Britain from the vast financial burden of an excessive overseas commitment after the Second World War was essential for the general improvement of living standards and the economic boom of the 1950s and 1960s at home and so benefited Britain as well as her former colonies.

Fourth, it is empirically unsustainable to liken a Europe dominated by Germany in 1918 as a European Union avant la lettre or to describe the European Union of today as a vehicle for the German domination of Europe. During the 1990s, when Ferguson and Charmley were writing, Germany was turned inward, absorbed in the unexpectedly gargantuan task of bringing East Germany into the modern world after the fall of the Berlin Wall. Talk of a "Fourth Reich" was alarmist fantasy; Germany since 1945 has been afraid of power, not still wedded to it. And in any case, the European Union is simply too large and complex an entity to sustain sweeping generalizations about German domination. Even describing it slightly more accurately as resting on the joint hegemony of Germany and France, on the Franco-German partnership, does not do it justice, least of all in the expanded European Union of twenty-eight nations, today, and certainly ignores the way in which key decisions have to be taken, through the Council of Ministers, with a single-country veto on many crucial issues. German financial policy has, it is true, imposed stringent austerity on southern European economies within the Eurozone, exporting its traumatic fears of inflation, derived from the experience of 1923, and there is a case to be made for a stronger element of reflation to stimulate economic growth. However, it is clear that this bears little or no resemblance to German plans in 1914 for the creation of a central European economic area under German domination, still less to the brutal methods of plunder and exploitation imposed on occupied countries by Nazi Germany in the 1940s. The Kaiser's European Union might well have been based on the territorially expanded Germany that the September Program and subsequent drafts of German war aims envisaged, not the much smaller Germany of today, and could have been bolstered by the imposition of an authoritarian and hierarchical system of rule, the denial of human rights to minorities, the curbing of trade unions and the enforced imposition of German customs and German institutions. We do not need to speculate about what the "New Order" in Europe meant under the Nazis: ruthless exploitation, mass murder, constant militarization. The one thing that can be said is that had the Nazis won World War II, it is highly unlikely that supposedly moderate and pragmatic elements like munitions minister Albert Speer would then have taken over and created a "New Order" that was more or less the same as the European Union later became; the EU was, and is, based on ideals of peace and compromise, both utterly foreign to Nazis, including Speer.[46]

Fifth, the counterfactual implicit in Charmley's claim that had Labour not come to power in 1945 and inaugurated the welfare state, Britain would have been more successful economically because a culture of enterprise would have replaced what became a culture of dependency, is implausible on a number of grounds. The Beveridge Report that provided the foundations for policy in this area was accepted not only by the Labour Party but also by the Conservatives, who made no attempt to reverse its consequences when they came to power in 1951. The war had generated a consensus behind the idea of a welfare state that transcended party boundaries.[47] Nor is there any evidence that this proved a hindrance to British economic performance, as postwar recovery was followed by the boom years of the late fifties and sixties. What changed the situation was the oil crisis of 1973, but while Mrs. Thatcher's liberalization of the economy, privatization of industry and utilities, and deregulation of banks in the 1980s created the conditions for another upturn in the economy, the downside of her reforms was starkly revealed as the credit crunch of 2009 inaugurated a crisis that was made much worse by the failure of successive governments to introduce proper regulation of the banking system so hastily liberalized a quarter of a century before. Here again, the grounds for a counterfactual are empirically too weak to sustain it.

So the British neutrality counterfactual does not stand up to close examination. To the versions proposed by Ferguson and Charmley can be opposed quite different versions proposed by others, by Addison, Roberts, Herwig, or Sansom. Historians customarily disagree about interpretations of the past, of course, but here we have disagreements not about interpretations but about actual facts, or rather, of course, about imagined facts. And therein lies the problem. All these authors posit long-term consequences from the changing of a single event. Imagined British neutrality in World War I or World War II has imagined consequences extending for several decades, right up to the end of the twentieth century. The trouble with counterfactual arguments used in this way is that far from liberating history from an imaginary straitjacket of Marxist determinism they confine it in another that in reality is far more constricting. This is because the counterfactual proposes an alternative future, in the sense of "what if A had happened instead of B?" then assumes or posits a whole series of other things that would have *inevitably* followed: "If A had happened instead of B, then *inevitably* C, D, and E would have followed, instead of what actually happened, namely, X, Y, and Z." But of course a thousand other things might, or would, have intervened to make this alternative course of events in practice completely unpredictable. If, for example, Britain had not entered the First World War, it is in practice completely inevitabilist to argue that this one change in the pattern of events would ineluctably have led to a whole chain of other events, from German victory in the First World War to the failure of Hitler to seize power and the retention of the British Empire all the way up to the end of the century. Chance and contingency are here eliminated altogether. Other factors extraneous to the limited question of relations between Britain and Germany are completely ignored, from the whole involvement and purposes of Germany in eastern Europe to the entire development of relations between the British colonizers and the Indian and African colonized. What would have occurred if other contingencies had intervened along the way? There is no way of knowing, but once you let the counterfactual genie out of the bottle, anything might happen.

Conditional statements of such hard-edged certainty are foreign to the historian's way of going about explanation, which is almost invariably tentative and involves considerable use of the word "probably." "Monocausal" explanations make historians uneasy; we prefer to pile up causes until events are overdetermined, that is, they have so many causes that if one did not operate the others would, and the event in question would still have occurred. The key of course lies in designating one cause as more operative than others. Historians usually construct hierarchies of causes — primary causes, secondary causes, main causes, subsidiary causes, and so on, which affect different parts of the explanation. If we are looking, for example, for causes of the First World War, we can say that the assassination of the heir to the Austro-Hungarian throne was a cause, but only of the Austrian ultimatum to Serbia (which had aided and abetted the assassins), and further, more important causal chains linking the Austro-Serbian conflict to wider European great-power rivalries needed to come into operation before the Austrian declaration of war on Serbia prompted a Russian declaration of war on Austria, a German declaration of war on Russia, and so on. British historians argued for some time that the principal cause of Britain's involvement in the war was the German invasion of Belgium, whose neutrality Britain had guaranteed, but this simplistic view is no longer very widely accepted, and historians instead look to other factors, from Anglo-German naval rivalry to the British policy of maintaining the balance of power on the European continent. In none of these explanations is it very helpful to start thinking about what might have happened if things had been otherwise—for example, if the Austrian heir to the throne had not been assassinated, if Serbia had fully and unconditionally accepted the Austrian ultimatum, if the Russians had held back, and so on. Our main interest is in putting together the chain of events, not in unpicking it. We know that the British cabinet debated seriously whether or not to enter the war, and that Foreign Secretary Grey's fears of a German-dominated Europe eventually won the day; we know this from the evidence of its deliberations, and we do not need any counterfactuals to help us understand how or why events took the course they did.

As Allan Megill has pointed out, the virtual historian usually has a starting point in real history, normally just before some momentous decision is made. Johannes Bulhof has helpfully noted that "counterfactuals are sentences that are of the form 'if *p* then *q*' where . . . the antecedent (the term following the 'if') is in fact false."[48] This moment of decision is conceptualized as a moment of contingency, when things might easily have gone in a different direction from the one they actually took, and what the counterfactual historian then does is to extrapolate history in one or other of those different directions. But this involves a huge range of assumptions about how history at that particular time, and in the following months, years, and sometimes centuries, operated. These assumptions necessarily eliminate contingency rather than underlining its importance and influence. As Megill notes, "contingency cuts two ways," for if we have contingency at the outset of a counterfactual speculation, then we must also have it in the early middle, the middle, and the late stages, indeed all the way through. Thus "contingency is not a train one can get on or off at will," so that counterfactual history in this sense "cannot follow any definable course at all. More precisely, it can follow a definable course only until the next contingency arises." It is thus not history but fiction, or "imaginative history."[49] In a similar way, Martin Bunzl suggests that in a counterfactual chain of reasoning, the prime condition of plausibility is undermined further with each successive step taken. For example, the counterfactual claim that if Al Gore had been elected president of the United States, America would not have invaded Afghanistan, elides numerous intermediate links in the counterfactual chain of reasoning, ending in a counterfactual conditional that is so remote from the initial false claim — the entirely plausible hypothesis that Al Gore might have won the election — that it cannot in any way carry conviction. Thus what Bunzl calls the consequent of a historical counterfactual is always the product of an act of imagination, unprovable because of the lack of evidence. He can only carry plausibility insofar as the imagination is disciplined by historical knowledge.[50]

This point has been made in various ways by many analysts of counterfactualism, including some of its practitioners. Jon Elster, for example, has pointed out that the reality created by an alternative timeline would be totally different from the actual timeline because everything is in reality connected; it is entirely artificial to select one element and leave everything else unchanged while we trace its imagined consequences from the original point of departure.[51] Because everything is connected, it is "arbitrary," as Steven Lukes notes, "to propose that counterfactual reasoning should be confined to imagining (a subclass of) possible antecedents — namely, those which the theory we use to infer the consequent tells us are compatible with the elements of the world that are not assumed to vary." Why should we not alter everything, he asks.[52] Similarly, the French writer Emmanuel Carrère concludes his discussion of counterfactuals by noting that "the trajectory of the counterfactualist cannot be a single line. . . . It is . . . a sequence of innumerable points, and in departing from each of these points, a multitude of possibilities freely radiates."[53]

Undermining his own contribution to *Virtual History*, Jonathan Clark points out:

> The contingent and the counterfactual are only congruent at the outset of any historical enquiry. Soon, they begin to pull in different directions. The counterfactual assumes

clearly identifiable alternative paths of development, whose distinctness and coherence can be relied on as the historian projects them into an unrealised future. An emphasis on contingency, by contrast, not only contends that the way in which events unfold followed no such path . . . it also entails that all counterfactual alternatives would themselves have quickly branched out into an infinite number of possibilities.[54]

A long-term counterfactual of the kind unfolded by Ferguson and Charmley, or even, in the case he himself discusses, namely, the proposition that if the American Revolution had not occurred in 1776 the French state would not have been overburdened by the financial cost of supporting it and so there would have been no French Revolution in 1789, is, as Clark notes, "so large, and so far removed from the actual outcome, that it loses touch with historical enquiry."[55] Statements such as the claim that had Britain stayed out of the First World War, then the German-dominated European Union would have been born much earlier than it was can never take the form of real retrospective predictions, since they do not specify the hundreds of intervening variables relevant to the prediction. In other words, the deployment of the what-if type of argument to posit a *long-term* alternative development assumes first, the nonexistence of any *further* contingencies and chances along the way, and second, the noninfluence of the *initial* alternative event, the first thing that didn't happen, on subsequent events in ways that could not be foreseen or predicted. All of this removes chance and contingency from history almost totally. Instead of restoring open futures to the past, it closes them off.

This is a point that two of the most sophisticated advocates of counterfactual history, Geoffrey Parker and Philip E. Tetlock, perhaps surprisingly, concede. In the conclusion to their volume *Unmaking the West*, they note that

those who subscribe to the view that history is for the most part "just one damned thing after another," with minimal interconnectedness among the various causes that shape events, should be especially wary of aggressive extrapolations of trends into counterfactual worlds. . . . By contrast, those who believe that there is a systemic logic to how history unfolds — be it a positive-feedback logic that propels us, ever accelerating, in a particular direction or a negative-feedback logic that keeps us locked into a particular present — should be more supportive of what-if speculations that aggressively lay out visions of distant hypothetical futures.[56]

Thus in their view, anyone who emphasizes the role of chance and contingency in history will put little faith in the utility of counterfactuals; only those who believe in teleology and determinism will find them useful. Yet in both cases the historians concerned are caught in a paradox. Believers in chance and contingency as the key factors in history cannot on this showing accept the plausibility or usefulness of counterfactuals; believers in teleology and determinism will not in any event feel the need to employ them.

Ferguson does not in the end claim that the British neutrality counterfactual helps us understand the decisions taken in 1914 and 1940. All he says is that "only by attempting to understand what would have happened had Britain stood aside can we be sure the right decision was made."[57] But the fact that Addison's counterfactual scenario, like Herwig's or Sansom's, is mainly a negative one points to the unavoidable conclusion that the positive counterfactual scenario painted by Ferguson, Charmley, and Clark is in the end little more than a rather obvious form of wishful thinking; rather than "what if," it's really little more than "if only." In this form it contributes nothing to our understanding of what actually did happen, because its concern is not really with examining how and why people like Sir Edward Grey or Winston Churchill took the decisions they took. Instead it's concerned with pointing up what are supposedly preferable alternatives and bemoaning the fact that they never came to pass. This kind of speculation is easy to do because, detached from the need to back arguments with actual, concrete evidence, it allows historians to rewrite history according to their present-day political purposes and prejudices. As Jonathan Clark warns: "Analysts of the counterfactual must beware of that easy escape which is offered by the argument that, but for some initial mistake, some tragic error, all would have been well, and mankind released from avoidable conflicts into a golden age of peaceful progress."[58] How that golden age might have looked is not a matter of informed counterfactual speculation but the product of purposive political motivation. Like the contributors to Daniel Snowman's collection *If I Had Been . . .* , Niall Ferguson and John Charmley and Alan Clark spend their time telling people in the past what they should have done, not trying to find out what they did and explain it. Wishful thinking is everywhere in the world of historical counterfactual. In all these cases, "the need for consolation," as Clark concludes, "overrides the desire for explanation."[59]

CHAPTER 3 *Future Fictions*

M any historical subjects have been treated counter-
factually. Novelists have been as wide-ranging in
their choice of topics as historians have. Often
their purposes, however, have been dramatically
different. Jorge Semprún's experimental novel *L'Algarabie*, published in 1981, for instance, sets its action in a world in which the
French president General de Gaulle has been killed in a helicopter
crash in 1975 and revolutionary movements of various kinds —
communist, anarchist, regionalist — run amok, leading to an all-
out civil war in which a new, ultra-left Paris Commune reaches
an agreement with the French government based at Versailles to
live and let live. Memories, identities, fact, fiction are all jumbled
together in a kaleidoscopic postmodernist presentation that constantly reminds the reader that what is being read is an artificial
construction. Paris becomes Berlin, as the characters go through
the wall encompassing the Commune at "Checkpoint Danny," a
playful reference both to the real "Checkpoint Charlie" through
which people could cross the Berlin Wall from the western sectors, and to Danny Cohn-Bendit, one of the real leaders of the
Parisian student revolt in 1968. Here the alterations flowing from
a single event — the death of President de Gaulle — rapidly leave
any recognizable historical path and become a phantasmagorical
product of the postmodernist imagination, and the point is not
to make any particular political or historical statement, but to
make the reader experience, and think about, the nature of narrative representation.[1]

Yet many if not most novelists who write counterfactual scenarios stick more closely to conventional linear narratives, with
the alteration of the historical context deriving, as in Semprún's
book, from a single alteration in historical reality, but the conse-

quences then unfolding in a deliberately logical way. Novelists who have based their fictions on counterfactual scenarios of this kind have tackled many subjects, often indulging in obvious fantasies of wishful thinking, like the Spanish authors who wrote stories in which the Republic rather than General Franco won the Civil War of 1936–39.[2] Particular national cultures have their own historical dramas and traumas, on which counterfactual fictions as well as nonfictions have tended to focus: the Revolution of 1789, the defeat of Napoleon in 1815, or the upheavals of 1968 for the French, the Civil War and the rule of General Franco for the Spanish, the failure of national pride in World War I and Mussolini's Fascist regime for the Italians, the Civil War and then the Vietnam War for the Americans, the early defeats in World War II for the British, the loss of World War I for the Germans; Catholics have written repeatedly and at length about the Protestant Reformation and the defeat of the Spanish Armada in sixteenth-century England and its political confirmation in the seventeenth century, from the failure of the Gunpowder Plot to the "Glorious Revolution" of 1688.

But the most popular subject by far has been the Nazi dictatorship in Germany. Imagining what things might have been like had the Nazis won the Second World War has been a popular pastime of novelists, television scriptwriters, and filmmakers as well as of historians for a long time. Why Nazism and not, say, Communism? Nazism occupies a central place in Western popular and public memory, as the embodiment of evil, the most extreme example of so many things civilization deplores, from racism and genocide to international aggression, warmongering, and dictatorship. Since 1945 at least, those who support it or believe in it have been a tiny, publicly reviled minority, whereas Soviet and other varieties of Communism have continued to command mass support, though in a dwindling number of parts of the world and mostly in a progressively diluted form. Because Soviet-style Communism continued in power in Europe up to 1990 and elsewhere even longer, there is little point in writing fantasies about what might have happened had Stalin not died in 1953, or had he invaded Western Europe in 1945: we know from decades of observation or experience how things would have been under his rule. As Aviezer Tucker has remarked, the popularity of fictional alternate histories focusing on "a world where the Nazis won the war . . . may be ascribed to an aesthetic fascination with apocalyptic landscapes, with consistent realistic depictions of a horrendous alternative universe, like a Bosch painting."[3]

Future fictions involving Nazism are overwhelmingly Anglo-American in provenance. Eighty percent of the list of 116 works of alternate histories of Nazism compiled by the American historian Gavriel Rosenfeld in 2011 have appeared in Britain or the United States.[4] The Anglo-American dominance of the genre may be because Britain and the United States were on the winning side in the Second World War, and so there is a sense of excitement generated by reminders of how narrow their escape from defeat perhaps was, and what a Nazi victory might have entailed. Portrayals of a world, including Britain and the United States, under Nazi domination reinforce the general, if occasionally disputed, conviction in these countries that the war was worth fighting. The global dominance of Hollywood, and the international cultural power of English-language literature, have also contributed to the hegemony of Anglo-American fictions about a future run by Nazis. Neither Britain nor the United States was occupied by a hostile power during the Second World War; by contrast, Germans, French, Russians, Italians, and other Europeans do not need fiction to remind them of the horrors of Nazi rule: they experienced it themselves in the most direct possible way (a similar point might be made about Japanese rule in China and the Pacific). As for the Germans, to imagine a world without Hitler is morally extremely risky; the element of wishful thinking would be all too obvious. To attribute the rise and triumph of Nazism to mere chance factors—an "industrial accident" to the motor of German history, as it has sometimes been called—looks too much like an excuse that lets the Germans off the hook, and so has always aroused fierce controversy in Germany itself whenever anybody has tried to do it. And, as Rosenfeld remarks, the playful element in future fictions of Nazism, and their role as popular entertainment, seem morally irresponsible and culturally shallow to a nation that rightly regards itself as bearing the prime responsibility for the Holocaust. Nevertheless, despite all this, fully 15 percent of the fictions in Rosenfeld's list are German in origin, testifying perhaps to a lingering ambivalence in German culture about the Nazis and what they did to the world, though in practice those German authors who have written in this genre have gone to some lengths to avoid giving Hitler any kind of *final* victory in their counterfactual narratives.[5]

Rosenfeld's list of alternate-history fictions includes 63 in which the Nazis win World War II, 29 in which Hitler escapes the bunker in 1945 and lives on elsewhere, and 18 in which Hitler never existed in the first place.[6] The predominance of depictions of a Nazi victory and its aftermath is not really surprising. Few of these narratives show any interest in trying to explain how or why the Nazis won, in sharp contrast to the many military-historical alternative histories of the Second World War. What novelists, film directors, and television producers are overwhelmingly interested in is the use of a Nazi-dominated postwar era as a backdrop for character and plot, setting fictional individuals in a nightmarish scenario that confronts them with stark moral choices and tangible, easily imaginable dangers. The locus classicus of such depictions is of course George Orwell's *1984*, which imagines a world dominated by indistinguishable totalitarian superpowers, modeled on Hitler's Third Reich and Stalin's Soviet Union, but owing rather more to Orwell's vision of the latter than to his memory of the former. In essence, Orwell's novel was a warning of what might happen in the future, if Britain and Europe succumbed to the Soviet threat, rather than an imaginary projection of an altered past, so in this sense, it is not really a counterfactual novel, any more than are the various novels about a Nazi-dominated future published in Britain before the war's end. Just like the future fictions of the early 1900s, such as Saki's *When William Came*, which describes a Britain groaning under the iron heel of the Kaiser, books like Martin Hawkins's *When Adolf Came* (London, 1943) were intended to stiffen British public resolve in the face of the German threat. Thus for example H. V. Morton's *I, James Blunt*, published in 1942 and presenting the diary entries of a British man living in the future in a Nazi-occupied England, was intended as a wake-up call, in Morton's words, to the "complacent optimists and wishful thinkers who . . . cannot imagine what life would be like if we lost the war."[7]

In the decade and a half after the war's end, only one fictional account of Britain under German occupation appeared — Noël Coward's play *Peace in Our Time*, a retrospective dramatic denunciation of appeasement and a celebration of British pluck, in which a resistance movement drives the Germans off the island despite the pusillanimity of collaborationists and defeatists; it belongs in spirit more to the wartime years than to the postwar world.[8] A more sophisticated depiction of a German victory on a general level was provided in 1950 by Randolph Robban's novel *Si l'Allemagne avait vaincu* (If Germany Had Won), a satirical account with its starting point in the Germans' deployment of the atom bomb, which they develop before anyone else, ending the war by dropping it on London and Chicago. Germany and Japan put Allied leaders on trial for war crimes (notably the bombing of their cities) and occupy the Soviet Union. But the relationship between the winners breaks down and they destroy each other in an atomic war. By reversing the signs, the pseudonymous author casts the conduct of the victorious Allies in a critical light with the aim of encouraging reconciliation between victor and vanquished in the postwar era.[9]

It was not until the 1960s that the next counterfactual publication emerged, the journalist Comer Clarke's *If the Nazis Had Come* (London, 1962). This used interviews with surviving German military leaders and genuine documentation of Nazi plans for the occupation of the British Isles to paint a grim picture of tyranny and oppression. This portrayal reflected not only the experience of occupied countries on the European continent, but also the theory of totalitarianism, pioneered by Orwell, that saw Nazi Germany (as well as Soviet Russia) as a monolithic dictatorship in which the leader imposed his will by force and people had no choice but to obey, unless they went underground and started a resistance movement. A similar scenario was developed in stories by the popular writer C. S. Forester, creator of the fictional seadog Horatio Hornblower, scourge of the French navy in the Napoleonic Wars, and the historian Hugh Thomas, among others. All these writers gave a good deal of space to developing the idea that German oppression would have sparked growing resistance, both reaffirming the validity of the war itself, and celebrating the bulldog spirit of the British people. As such, they were still recognizably part of the genre of wartime future fictions. They were published in a postwar era in which the Churchillian ethos was invoked in order to bolster British morale at a time of austerity at home and decline abroad, symbolized by the disastrous British defeat in the brief war over the Suez Canal in 1956.[10]

These works ran in tandem with a stream of war movies, including *The Dam Busters* (1955), *Reach for the Sky* (1956), *Sink the Bismarck* (1960), *Ill Met by Moonlight* (1957), *The Battle of the River Plate* (1956), and many more, that not only celebrated the martial character of the British but also legitimized the hierarchical society in which they lived, with the officer class, complete with stiff upper lip and clipped English accents, effectively commanding a compliant and deferential working class rank-and-file in the struggle for decency and order. In these depictions, the ordinary German military or naval officer appeared as fundamentally decent, reflecting the British experience of the war on the Western Front and in North Africa; only the Nazis were portrayed as brutal characters undermining the laws of war and the fundamental principles of honor and correctness in dealing with an enemy. Even in wartime and early postwar British representations of Germany, therefore, not all Germans were irredeemably wicked. But by the mid-1960s, hierarchy and deference were coming into question as a new, postwar generation reached maturity, affluence and materialism took hold in British culture, and the "swinging sixties" proclaimed a new ethos of personal freedom and rebellion. Simultaneously, a very public reconciliation with Germany and the Germans, symbolized in Queen Elizabeth II's state visit to West Germany in 1965, allowed a larger role for the "good Germans" in fictional representations of the Third Reich. In the Federal Republic of Germany, younger historians began to produce sophisticated studies of the social history of the Nazi years, uncovering the chaotic and factionalized structures of the Nazi regime and demonstrating the possibility of dissent from it among many sectors of German society. With détente, totalitarianism theory gave way to a more differentiated approach. The complex and sensitive issue of longer-term continuities reaching back from Hitler to the Kaiser and beyond was raised by the German historian Fritz Fischer's study of German aims in World War I. Much of this new German work was translated into English or publicized by a new generation of British historians working on German history.[11]

All this created a new context in which counterfactual explorations of a world, and specifically a Britain, in which the Nazis had won World War II, became more interesting and more attractive to writers and filmmakers. British novels, plays, films, and television dramas from the mid-1960s through the 1970s and 1980s reflected this context by imagining a Britain in which the occupying Germans might not have been uniformly brutal or generally resisted. British collaborators featured as characters in Giles Cooper's TV drama *The Other Man* (1964), Kevin Brownlow's film of the same year *It Happened Here*, Philip Mackie's three-part TV drama *An Englishman's Castle*, broadcast in 1978, and other fictions up to and including Len Deighton's novel *SS-GB*, published in the same year. The most notable depiction of Britain under Nazi rule was by the popular historian Norman Longmate, who in 1972 published a book (to go with a television documentary) with the title *If Britain Had Fallen: The Real Nazi Occupation Plans.* The book was based securely on a mixture of actual German preparations and plans for the occupation of Britain, and on the known experience of the actual German occupation of the one part of Britain the Nazis did manage to take over, the Channel Isles, just off the French coast. Longmate thus claimed to describe "not merely what *might* have happened but *probably would* have happened."[12]

In Longmate's scenario the Royal Air Force loses the Battle of Britain, paving the way for a full-scale invasion: the essential precondition for all his other speculations. The king flees to Canada while Winston Churchill is killed fighting the invaders. After his death, the British more or less give up. Searching for a Quisling, a politician to head a puppet government, the Nazis hit upon Sir Samuel Hoare, named in the real prewar diaries of Sir Alexander Cadogan, a senior diplomat, as a likely candidate. Hoare had negotiated a pact with the French giving Mussolini what he wanted in Abyssinia and would probably take the same line in dealing with the Germans. Thirty-two years later, however, when he came to reissue the book, Longmate changed his mind and thought that the British Fascist leader Sir Oswald Mosley was the likeliest candidate for prime minister. Mosley himself claimed after the war that he would have committed suicide rather than do such a thing, but he was still in politics at this time and his word cannot be trusted. As for the new head of state: "Wherever one looks, in Great Britain or the United States, the Duke of Windsor's name emerges as the likeliest head of a pro-Nazi government." He might well have occupied the throne in the belief that he could mitigate the worst excesses of Nazi rule, and his vain wife might have been seduced by the promise of being called "Your Majesty" (the British royal family would not even allow her to be called "Your Royal Highness").[13]

Drawing on actual Nazi plans, Longmate has the occupiers take down Nelson's column in Trafalgar Square and cart it off to Berlin. The Nazis loot and ransack everything in sight, expropriating Jewish property and taking from museums and galleries cultural objects they regard as German and shipping off petrol and other basic supplies for the use of the German armed forces. The Gestapo would have arrested known anti-Nazis (a somewhat arbitrary list) and banned suspicious organizations including the Salvation Army. Many aspects of everyday life would have continued more or less unchanged, though as they did in every other country they occupied, the Germans would have made the British drive on the right. Large numbers of young British men would have been sent to Germany as forced laborers, and the 450,000 members of the Jewish community would have been rounded up and sent to the gas chambers of Auschwitz. Before the invasion, as we know, the British military authorities had organized "auxiliary units" to harass the enemy by sabotage and guerilla warfare in the event of an invasion, but they would not have lasted long and their activities would have prompted savage reprisals. "Resistance" would most likely have taken the form of sullen noncooperation, but collaboration would also have been limited. The nightmare would have ended with the Americans dropping an atomic bomb, or bombs, on Germany and crossing the Atlantic to liberate the oppressed Europeans.[14]

Longmate's book was published against a backdrop of a new wave of writing and broadcasting about Britain, Germany, and the war that lasted from the mid-sixties to the late eighties. It focused on satirizing the "stiff upper lip" and the celebration of British military prowess, as in the popular television comedy show *Dad's Army*, which aired from 1968 to 1977. The assault on the hierarchical society and self-congratulatory myths of the 1950s was liberating in many ways, but it also led to a widespread debate in the 1970s about the "decline of Britain," in which the loss of empire, the inefficiency and inadequacy of British institutions, and the relative retardation of the British economy in comparison to the German, caused a bout of national soul-searching that culminated in the radical reforms of Prime Minister Thatcher's Conservative government after 1979. During this debate, questioning the determination of the British to resist German domination in the event of an invasion in the past became a metaphorical way of underlining the supposed weakness and inadequacy of British institutions in the present. Thus a series of authors followed Longmate in arguing that some Britons at least would have collaborated with the occupying forces.[15]

At the same time, the humanization of the German invaders went along with a widespread admiration in the 1970s for the supposed German qualities of efficiency, hard work, and entrepreneurship that the British would do well to emulate. The German automobile company Audi's slogan *Vorsprung durch Technik* was used regularly, untranslated, in advertisements on British television and clearly had a wider message to convey. The popular situation comedy *Auf Wiedersehen, Pet* described British bricklayers, facing unemployment or low wages in their own country, finding work and fulfillment on German construction sites. In the eighties, however, things began to change. The celebration of Britain's role in the Second World War was revived dramatically in Britain's successful military operation to recover the Falkland Islands in the South Atlantic from a brutal military dictatorship in Argentina, which invaded them in 1982. After this, the Thatcher government turned to confronting the trade unions, dubbed by her as "the enemy within," leading to scenes of unprecedented violence as phalanxes of police charged lines of picketing miners. The linguistic ground was being laid for the reemergence of an older way of talking about Britain, one shorn of the complexities and ambiguities it had acquired since the 1960s.

At the end of the 1980s, the language of the Second World War was applied to a new subject as German reunification aroused deep hostility in some members of Mrs. Thatcher's government, led by the prime minister herself, who made clear her fear of a resurgence of German power in a "Fourth Reich," dominating Europe through the European Community and its successor the European Union. As Mrs. Thatcher became rapidly more hostile to the EU, growing numbers of Conservative MPs and writers followed her in identifying it as a vehicle for a renewed German bid for supremacy. Within a remarkably short space of time, Mrs. Thatcher was ousted from power by a revolt among the pragmatists in her cabinet, but the damage had been done: Euroscepticism was born. As books and articles attacking the Germans as unrepentant Nazis poured off the presses, public opinion swung rapidly in an anti-German direction. The average score awarded to the Germans in respect of friendliness fell among British respondents to opinion poll questioning from 12.7 percent in 1990 to −38.8 percent in 1994. An average of 26 percent agreed that Germany would be a nice place for them to work in 1990, but only 5 percent thought so six years later. Twenty-six percent of British respondents regarded the Germans as Britain's best friend in 1987, but only 9 percent did in 1992, when no fewer than 53 out of every 100 Britons considered Nazism could reemerge in Germany compared to 23 percent five years previously.[16] These figures stood in stark contrast to survey data from other European countries, where attitudes toward Germany remained largely unchanged. This shift in the British public mood was reinforced by the many fiftieth anniversary commemorations of World War II that took place in these years, from the outbreak of the war, marked in 1989, through the Battle of Britain in 1990 to the Battle of El Alamein in 1993 and VE-Day in 1995.

The language of World War II was taken up in the new Eurosceptic discourse most obviously by the Conservative MP William Cash, in his book *Against a Federal Europe: The Battle for Britain*, published in 1991. The subtitle already suggested a rerun of the Second World War, with its echoes of the Battle of Britain. This time, however, it was William Cash who reached for the skies in search of his finest hour. From the very outset, as in 1940, there is no doubt in Cash's book about who the enemy is. "Britain," Cash warns on page 1, "could become a mere province in a Europe dominated by Germany." "The German attitude to Europe," he warned, "is . . . determined by a massive historical heritage." A more closely integrated Europe would in Cash's view be "a greater Germany, balancing uneasily between East and West, inheriting and perhaps magnifying the complexes and instabilities of post-Bismarckian Germany." Everyone knew the catastrophes to which the instabilities of post-Bismarckian Germany led in 1914, 1933, 1939 and 1945. A German-dominated, closely integrated European Union would not last very long, and, Cash implied, chaos and violence would be the result of its dissolution.[17] Conservative historians joined in the chorus of denunciation of the EU as a vehicle of German domination. "How long," John Charmley asked, commenting on German reunification, "before Germany decides that it is too big for the boots it is allowed to wear — and who could stop it this time if it decides to get a bigger pair?" This seemed on the face of it to run counter to Charmley's previously expressed view that it would have been reasonable and indeed desirable for the British government to have reached a separate peace with Germany in 1940. For in view of what he wrote in 1995, how could Charmley suppose that the Germans could have been relied upon to keep their promises in 1940?[18]

Nevertheless, Charmley's new views were shared by other historians on the right. The emergence of Euroscepticism, couched in the rhetoric of World War II and using a manufactured public memory of Britain's finest hour to target Germany as the proxy for Brussels, formed the essential context for the counterfactual speculations developed by Charmley and Ferguson in particular as they asserted that Britain should have remained in "splendid isolation" from the travails of the Continent in 1914 and 1940, thus saving the British Empire and preventing the Holocaust. In these works, the German domination of the EU is taken as a given, and described in alternative scenarios as having been achieved without war or conflict already in 1915. Yet the image of a Britain safely isolated from Europe was wishful Eurosceptic thinking that clashed starkly with what Eurosceptics perceived to be the terrible reality of the 1990s, in which the Fourth Reich was threatening to overwhelm the UK yet again, so that counterfactual depictions of a peaceful development of continental European unity in an imagined past shorn of British participation in the two World Wars had to be pushed to one side to make way for the deployment of rhetoric derived from World War II to deal with the perceived threat posed by an allegedly aggressive and expansionist Germany in the present.[19]

Counterfactual history picked up the new-old rhetoric of defiance and argued that collaboration in the event of a German occupation of Britain would have been minimal. Attacking a study by the liberal *Guardian* journalist Madeleine Bunting,[20] which argued that contrary to their self-generated myth, a myth accepted by earlier writers like Longmate, the populace of the Channel Islands had not only failed to resist the Nazi occupiers but also collaborated with them all the way up to helping them deport the islands' Jews to Auschwitz, Andrew Roberts pointed out that, contrary to what Bunting claimed, the Channel Islands were a poor model on which to base generalizations on this topic, since a third of their adult male population had been evacuated, the Germans stationed 37,000 troops on islands inhabited by 60,000 people, the islanders had a tradition of obeying authority, there were no strong trade unions or political parties, and there were neither mountainous areas nor big cities in which to base a resistance movement. The islanders were half French anyway, said Roberts, and the British were far more loyal to their country than the French were to theirs. Pacifism, which had briefly flourished before the war, was effectively dead. There was no Nazi "fifth column" of collaborators and subversives in Britain. The Duke of Windsor, argued Roberts, might have been persuaded to take the throne after Churchill had been killed resisting the invaders and King George VI had left for Canada, and a pro-Nazi politician like Lloyd George might have been persuaded to become prime minister, as might Sir Samuel Hoare, though not Mosley, whom the Germans knew to be unpopular (though this consideration had not stopped them elevating the even more unpopular Vidkun Quisling in Norway). The arch-appeaser R. A.

Butler, another proponent of a separate peace, might have eased the Germans' task by collaborating. But these would have been exceptions, and Roberts asserted boldly that had the Germans occupied Britain, "they would then have been faced with the implacable, visceral enmity of a nation in arms."[21] The Eurosceptic message of his article was rammed home in his discussion of the line that would be taken by the Nazi-controlled British press: "The emphasis which Vichy propagandists placed on a common European future as the catalyst by which honour and self-respect could be restored would have been repeated word for word in Britain."[22]

Roberts's counterfactual vision of a Britain rising up in national rage against a German occupation carried out in the name of Europe was echoed a few years later by Owen Sheers's *Resistance*, which depicted an active resistance movement continuing to fight the occupying Germans despite the collaborationism of a new government headed by R. A. Butler under the guidance of the restored King Edward VIII, pledging "to bridge the differences between Britain and Germany and build towards a united Europe, standing strong against the capitalist Americans in the West and the Bolsheviks in the East."[23] More immediately, Roberts's Eurosceptic counterfactuals were paralleled by his futuristic novel *The Aachen Memorandum*, published in 1995. This political fiction is set in an imaginary future around the middle of the twenty-first century, when Britain has been fully incorporated into a German-dominated federal European Union. The British monarchy has long since emigrated to New Zealand, and students are now expelled from Oxford for proposing the loyal toast at dinner. Britain has been broken up into a series of provinces. A plethora of European directives governs everyday life. "Classlessness legislation" has forced the renaming of Earl's Court, while sexual intercourse is governed by directives on harassment and on health and hygiene. Nelson has been taken off the school syllabus during the "depatriation" of the history curriculum, and his statue on the column in Trafalgar Square, now renamed Delors Square, after the president of the European Commission, has been replaced by one of Robert Schuman, the founder of the European Union. Labor directives ensure that managers are at the beck and call of works councils. Corruption is everywhere, especially at the top.[24] Everyday life in Britain is now governed by "federal fashion," "federal" has become slang for "good" or "fashionable"), which dictates that women should have hairy armpits like the Germans, and men should, horror of horrors, kiss each other twice on each cheek when they meet. Continental-style trams have largely replaced cars and buses on the streets of London, making previously quick and simple journeys endlessly long and complicated (it has to be said that of all the imaginary predictions in the book, this is one of the most implausible). A European directive has forced the British to drive on the right, causing mass carnage on the roads, and a federal police force, Europol, behaves much as the Gestapo would have done had Britain been occupied by the Nazis. German is the only foreign language taught in schools. All this, as the book's hero, inevitably called Horatio, reveals, reflects the fact that the "Germans . . . pretty much run the union" and call it the "Reich . . . among themselves when they don't think anyone is listening." Needless to say, Horatio leads a resistance movement that eventually destroys the hated rule of the Continental foreigners.[25]

The Aachen Memorandum occupies an intermediate place between predictive novels warning the British public of dire consequences should present policies not be changed, such as *When William Came* or *When Adolf Came*, and counterfactual imaginings of how Britain might have looked had the Nazis occupied the country in the 1940s, imaginings on which the novel freely draws. True counterfactual fiction in the Eurosceptic vein in the 1990s was exemplified by Robert Harris's novel *Fatherland* (London, 1992). Set not in Britain but in Germany, in the year 1964, the novel tells the story of a detective (and member of the SS) whose investigation of a string of murders leads him to uncover a government attempt to eliminate the principal surviving perpetrators of the Holocaust and destroy all remaining evidence for it so as not to jeopardize relations with the United States, whose president is about to come on a state visit. Harris knew his way around the historiography of Nazi Germany, and one of the book's most striking features is its accurate depiction of what Berlin ("Germania") might have looked like after a successful world war. *Fatherland* had a strong Eurosceptical subtext. As Harris stated in an article published to mark the novel's appearance, "I spent four years writing . . . a novel about a fictional German superpower, and, as I wrote, it started turning into fact. . . . One does not have to share the views of . . . Margaret Thatcher to note the similarity between what the Nazis planned for western Europe and what, in economic terms, has come to pass."[26] The message was underlined by the depiction in the novel of British and American collaborationism with Nazism, as the United Kingdom is led by the restored pro-Nazi monarch King Edward VIII while the appeaser and defeatist former U.S. ambassador in London, Joseph Kennedy, has become American president. Exciting, suspenseful, and well written, the novel was an instant best seller. But also, as Rosenfeld remarks: "In part, *Fatherland*'s commercial success in Britain reflected the novel's ability to exploit British uncertainty about a reunified Germany and the desirability of European integration."[27]

The novel took its cue from the fall of numerous East European dictatorships at the end of the 1990s to suggest that even a victorious Third Reich would have been a fragile structure, unlikely to outlive Hitler, and rapidly declining from its original vigor and aggression, doomed to eventual collapse and disintegration. Harris, like C. J. Sansom in his 2012 novel *Dominion*, whose debt to *Fatherland* is explicit, follows mainstream historiography in emphasizing the divided and unstable nature of the Nazi regime.[28] In some respects, however, the counterfactual scenarios on which the two novels are based diverge quite strikingly. Thus, for example, unlike other writers, Sansom does not think that the pro-Nazi ex-king Edward VIII would have been restored in the place of his brother George VI, since most Britons had not forgiven him for abdicating in the first place, and the Germans knew him to be "such an irresponsible and foolish man that, as King, he would have been a headache to any government."[29] In other parts of Europe, however, the Nazis had no such scruples or reservations about appointing unpopular collaborators, such as the fascist leader Ante Pavelić in Croatia, and it seems unlikely, in view of what became his real wartime record, that George VI would have remained in Britain when it became a Nazi client state, though one can never be quite sure. A more serious objection to the idea of the Duke of Windsor as a Nazi puppet monarch would lie in the difficulty the Nazis would experience in actually laying hands on his person. Churchill and the British government were concerned to get him out of the way, moving him first to Portugal then to the Bahamas, and it is likely they would have made every effort to keep him from falling into the hands of the Nazis.

More seriously, however divided and disputatious the Nazi leadership may have been, Harris's scenario departs quite a long way from what is historically plausible in depicting a postwar, peacetime Europe living under a stable German domination. In fact, many historians would agree that war for the Nazis was not only war without limit, it was also war without end. In his long unpublished *Second Book* written in 1928, and on subsequent occasions too, Hitler made it clear that the purpose of conquering Eastern Europe was not only to provide Germany with a source of food supplies that would enable her to avoid the kind of Allied blockade that had done such damage in the First World War, but also to give her a land empire equivalent to that of the United States, a land empire that in the long run would provide the basis for a greater war, between Germany and America. Even assuming, therefore, that the Germans could have destroyed the Soviet Union — such a large "if" that Sansom, for example, has the Wehrmacht and the Red Army still slugging it out in the 1950s without any concrete result — it is unlikely that peace would have come. As the historian Tim Mason noted: "Whatever one makes of Hitler's speculations before 1941 about a future war of world domination against the United States, the conquest of 'living space' in European Russia was never even conceived of as being a finite goal, and Hitler ruminated repeatedly about the danger of degeneration setting in, if the German people should ever find themselves in a situation in which they did not have to struggle against adversaries."[30] For his scenario to be plausible, Harris has to add to the unlikely eventuality of the Nazis ever agreeing to bring the war to an end the postulate of Hitler actually fighting the Americans to a stalemate and concluding a peace agreement with them. Everything we know about Hitler strongly suggests that he was never willing to compromise, and, as he said, always "went for broke"; for him it could only ever be victory or death, the triumph of the will or utter annihilation, nothing in between. And in practice, the enormous disparity in resources between Germany and the United States would have made it unlikely that war between them would have resulted in a stalemate, even had the Third Reich conquered Britain and concluded peace with the Soviet Union (another unlikely scenario).[31] The changed conditions necessary to underpin Harris's fantasy are just too numerous and too large to make it plausible as counterfactual history, even in the form of fiction.

The emergence of Eurosceptic counterfactualism in Britain in the 1990s undermines Gavriel Rosenfeld's argument that over the long haul, a process of "normalization" has taken place in the British view of Hitler and Nazism, expressed in the changing character of future fictions, as Nazism ceased to be a simple object of moral opprobrium linked to a self-congratulatory representation of Allied resistance to it, and attitudes to, and representations of, a counterfactual Nazi future became more complex and more self-critical. Rosenfeld repeats this argument through his book at every possible stage like a mantra.[32] But it is a massive oversimplification. It is given the lie by the sharp deterioration of British attitudes toward Germany in the 1990s, which led to a merging of Nazis and Germans in Eurosceptic rhetoric, and prompted a new wave of fictions and speculations about what Europe would have looked like had the Nazis won. Because this dramatic worsening of British attitudes to Germany and the German past does not fit into Rosenfeld's thesis, he simply ignores it.[33] The fact is, moreover, that the concept of "normalization" is fundamentally meaningless—what is "normal" is normal only in a given historical context: fear of a European future dominated by evil Nazis was normal in Britain during the Second World War, just as the belief that such a future had in many respects already happened, or was about to happen, was normal in British Eurosceptic narratives of the 1990s. Moreover, "normalization" is itself a predictive concept: the implication is that once things have become "normal," they will always remain so in the future. It is thus metaphysical rather than historical, untestable by empirical investigation.

The way in which the concept of "normalization" smooths over changes of attitude in other countries is evident in Rosenfeld's narrative too. Few things are less convincing in his book than the claim that the 1990s saw a "declining German belief in the power of memory and the possibility of justice," or a "desire to normalize the memory of the Nazi past."[34] For the 1990s, following the fall of the Berlin Wall, the collapse of Communism, and the reunification of the two Germanys, East and West, was on the contrary a decade that saw the resumption of war crimes trials across Europe, the highlighting of the Holocaust in public memory in Europe and the United States, the global impact of Steven Spielberg's movie *Schindler's List*, the opening of Holocaust memorial museums in many countries, the conversion of neglected German concentration camp sites into centers of remembrance and education, the placing of a memorial to Nazism's Jewish victims at the center of Germany's new capital city, Berlin, the uncovering of the complicity in Nazi crimes of many German institutions, from the armed forces to the medical profession, and later on the Foreign Office and its diplomats, and much more besides.[35] The problem with Rosenfeld's analysis is not simply that it relies on the crude and ultimately redundant concept of "normalization"; it also fails to set alternative histories — real and fictional — in their proper historical context, a context that, far from pursuing a single, predictable linear development toward the "normal," underwent, and is still undergoing, many unpredictable twists and turns over time.

This context is evident in the numerous postwar attempts to imagine a world in which Hitler had somehow managed to escape from his Berlin bunker in 1945 and survive into the postwar era. A large number of these fictions, particularly in the United States, have focused on making up for the frustration felt by many that Hitler had not been personally brought to account for his crimes. Books such as Philippe van Rjndt's *The Trial of Adolf Hitler* (New York, 1978), David B. Charnay's *Operation Lucifer: The Chase, Capture and Trial of Adolf Hitler* (London, 2001), which owes a good deal to van Rjndt's earlier book, James Marino's *The Asgard Solution* (New York, 1983), and Joseph Heywood's *The Berkut* (New York, 1987), engage in this wish fulfillment, as do, in a rather different way, numerous B movies and comic-book stories that depict the dangers of not bringing a surviving Hitler to trial. In this way, stories of Hitler's survival were inserted into a political critique of the relative failure of governments across the world to bring old Nazis to justice, a critique that became particularly noticeable after the revival of war crimes trials in the 1960s, with the Eichmann trial in Jerusalem in 1961 and the Auschwitz trials in Frankfurt in 1964.[36] By contrast, the critic George Steiner's strange short novel *The Portage to San Cristóbal of A. H.* (London, 1981) seems to have been intended as an attack on the obsession with Hitler that had become notable in the previous few years with the appearance of books, movies, and television programs about the Nazis in what had become known as the "Hitler-wave." Hitler, surviving in the South American jungle, was, Steiner suggested, an irrelevance in the late twentieth century. Instead of constantly recalling him to mind, people, especially Jews, should forget about him so they could face the future with more confidence and more optimism.[37]

Rather different is the recent wave of books claiming that Hitler (and, usually, Eva Braun) really did escape the bunker after faking their deaths. Such books claim to be based in reality, and sometimes on serious historical research. The vogue was begun by a British surgeon, W. Hugh Thomas, who attracted considerable attention with a book, published in 1995, purporting to demonstrate that the charred human remains found in the Reich Chancellery garden, above the Berlin bunker, in 1945, were not those of Hitler and Eva Braun. Thomas presented a considerable quantity of seemingly plausible forensic evidence, and his credentials as a medical expert added to his credibility. However, he had already claimed some years earlier that Rudolf Hess, the former deputy leader of the Nazi Party imprisoned for life at the Nuremberg war crimes trial in 1945, and incarcerated in the fortress at Spandau, just outside Berlin, was not in fact who he seemed to be, but someone else; and in 2001 he similarly claimed that SS leader Heinrich Himmler, whom eyewitnesses recorded as having committed suicide in 1945 after being arrested and recognized by British troops, was actually someone else too.[38] Clearly Thomas had too much of a habit of discovering unlikely doubles, and the more he added to his list, the less plausible his theories became. To have sustained these deceptions would have required conspiracies on a considerable scale, and at the latest with his book on Himmler, it became clear that despite their apparently serious examinations of the medical evidence, Thomas's books lacked any historical or forensic credibility.

Thomas did not have much to say about what happened to the real Hess, Hitler, Braun, or Himmler, but this gap in the literature was imaginatively filled by a number of other works published after the turn of the new century, including, for example, Ron T. Hansig's *Hitler's Escape* (London, 2005). And considerable media interest was created by a recently published investigation by two journalists, Gerrard Williams and Simon Dunstan.

On 11 April 2013, in one of many similar media stories report-
ing on the book and on plans to turn it into a television program, a reporter from the *Sun* newspaper, writing from Argentina, noted:

> Sensational claims have recently re-surfaced that Nazi
> Führer Adolf Hitler escaped his fate in his Berlin bunker and
> lived out his old age here in the wilds of Patagonia. Contro-
> versial book *Grey Wolf, The Escape Of Adolf Hitler*, by British
> authors Gerrard Williams and Simon Dunstan, published in
> October, describes how Hitler and wife Eva Braun even had
> two daughters who were still alive around a decade ago. They
> insist Hitler and Braun escaped the bunker in a secret tunnel
> and were replaced by doubles who committed suicide. And
> they claim it was the burned bodies of these doubles that
> were discovered by the avenging Red Army. In what the au-
> thors call "the greatest sleight of hand in history" Hitler and
> Braun then escaped to Argentina in a submarine before set-
> ting up home in a remote hideaway close to Bariloche. Here,
> so the theory goes, the tormented Führer spent his time plot-
> ting the emergence of a Fourth Reich before dying at 73 in
> 1962, his remains cremated and scattered.
>
> The evidence, the authors were reported to have told the
> *Daily Mail* on 28 October 2011, was "overwhelming," and
> they told Sky News: "We didn't want to re-write history,
> but the evidence we've discovered about the escape of Adolf
> Hitler is just too overwhelming to ignore. There is no for-
> ensic evidence for his, or Eva Braun's deaths, and the stories
> from the eyewitnesses to their continued survival in Argen-
> tina are compelling."

The problem was, of course, as critics pointed out, that the authors' endnotes became vague or were missing altogether when it
came to supporting crucial claims and allowing readers to check
them. In addition, the mass of genuine evidence for the bodies
outside the bunker being Hitler's and Eva Braun's — including

Hitler's teeth, verified against his dental records — was passed over or sweepingly dismissed, along with the numerous eyewitness accounts by members of his entourage gathered immediately after the war by Hugh Trevor-Roper and published in his book *The Last Days of Hitler* (London, 1947). Finally, the authors had failed altogether to follow up their belief that Hitler and Eva Braun had been survived by two daughters living in Argentina. Once again, the theory depended on the postulate of a vast conspiracy to suppress the truth, extending over many decades and involving hundreds if not thousands of professional historians, eyewitnesses, archives, officials, investigators, journalists and many more. It did not say much for the authors' opinion of the historical profession that they dismissed its established research as the product either of deliberate deception or of a woeful failure to inquire properly after the truth.

Spurious historical investigations of this kind are closely related in methodological terms to the politically motivated phenomenon of Holocaust denial, in which considerable forensic ingenuity is devoted to attempting to prove that six million Jews were not killed by the Nazis during the Second World War, that there were no gas chambers at Auschwitz, that Hitler did not have a plan or program to kill the Jews, and that the evidence that historians have put together to demonstrate that these things actually did happen has been concocted by a Jewish-led conspiracy after the war. If writers like Thomas, or Williams and Dunstan, are relatively innocent of political motivation in their intent, the same certainly cannot be said of the Holocaust deniers, who are generally driven by antisemitic, racist, neo-Nazi, or Islamist extremist ideology, and use their research — often decked out with all the panoply of footnoted scholarship and conducted in serious-sounding centers with names like "The Institute of Historical Review" — to try and persuade people that there is a vast and sinister Jewish conspiracy controlling the mass media, the historical profession, governments, universities, and political parties, forcing them all to suppress the truth and ruling the world in its own interests.[39]

This kind of conspiracy theory, often based on claims that established knowledge is "official" knowledge and therefore to be mistrusted, could be found in an even more extreme form, if that can be believed, in works such as M. Robert K. Teske, Jr.'s *The Omega Files: The Military-Industrial/Nazi/Alien Connection and the Infiltration of America by the Fourth Reich* (New York, 2012). The book's publicity blurb stated:

> What you are about to read is controversial, and may be offensive to some audiences. Reader discretion is advised. (NOTE: In the usage of the word "Alien" feel free to substitute it with "Demonic," "Fallen Angel," "Supernatural" or "Occult" as any of those words would aptly apply within the contents of this manuscript.) . . . If, as the late J. Allen Hynek claimed, over 1 in 40 people have been abducted and "processed" by the "alien/secret government" agenda—or 1 in 10 according to more recent sources—then you are bound to know SOMEONE who is an abductee and KNOWS it. This information is for THEM. For those who are not "UFO Abductees," the information in this file is nevertheless vital and applicable, and may one day save your life!!! . . . This file contains the most intricate and intimate details of a global conspiracy which seems to be rooted in an alien—military—industrial collaboration which is intent on bringing all freedom-loving peoples of this world under its control, through the implementation of a global government which has commonly been referred to as the "New World Order."

The book claims that flying saucers were built by the Nazis before the end of the war, and used to escape by the leaders of the Third Reich, who then hid themselves in underground bunkers in various parts of the world, including Antarctica, from where they were trying to establish the "New World Order."

Fantastic though such ideas seem, an opinion survey conducted by Public Policy Polling at the end of March 2013 found that "28 percent of American voters believe that a secretive power elite with a globalist agenda is conspiring to eventually rule the world through an authoritarian world government, or New World Order." Twenty-nine percent believe aliens exist, and 21 percent believe a UFO crashed at Roswell, New Mexico, in 1947, and the U.S. government covered it up.[40] Beliefs such as these are more prevalent among Republicans than among Democrats (only 15 percent of whom believe in the New World Order theory, though, puzzlingly, 6 percent of them also believe that Barack Obama is the Antichrist, a far lower figure than the 20 percent of Republicans who hold this view, but surprising nonetheless). They act as a metaphorical expression of extreme distrust in government, which is equated symbolically with evil forces such as Nazism. Such distrust goes hand in hand with a belief that government and its supposedly officially endorsed research publications, as purveyed, for example, by university academics and researchers, are deliberately suppressing the truth, to which only a few privileged individuals such as Teske, Hansig, Thomas, Williams and Dunstan, or Holocaust deniers of various kinds, have real access thanks to the depth of their research or the acuity of their insight. Speculative or pseudohistories and fictions such as these clearly differ from counterfactual histories and fictions, though they are also clearly related to them. They claim to present not alternatives to what actually happened, but real representations of genuine historical truth. But the line between the two is thin and often difficult to discern.

Thus, to take an obvious example, the science fiction writer Philip K. Dick's novel *The Man in the High Castle* (New York, 1962) is set in an imaginary world after a war which the Nazis and the Japanese have won, dividing the spoils, particularly North America, between them. At the same time, however, the eponymous character has actually written a counterfactual novel, *The Grasshopper Lies Heavy*, which represents a different version of reality in which the Germans and Japanese have lost the war, Hitler has been captured, tried, and condemned, the British Empire has survived, and the Nationalists have defeated the Communists in China. At the end of the book, the characters discover that *The Grasshopper Lies Heavy* depicts the truth, and they themselves are fictional.[41] From here it is only a short step to science-fiction narratives in which time's arrow has been bent by circumstance, but can be straightened out by time travelers going back to the original event to set things to rights. In such novels, the author often goes to some lengths to present a correctly realized scenario, for instance, with the still-functioning Inquisition behaving in a twentieth-century England that is still Catholic following the victory of the Spanish Armada in 1688 in much the same way as it did in early modern Spain.[42] Yet science-fiction writers are liable to introduce into such narratives completely unhistorical or even impossible plot devices such as futuristic technology, laser guns, time machines, and the like, taking the reader a long way from the counterfactual starting point.[43]

The real and the fictional thus blend, as they do in many alternative histories that posit the survival of Hitler into the postwar world, or indeed the rather smaller number that try to imagine a world in which he had died before coming to power, or survived but failed to become German chancellor. For the most part, such fictions are classic examples of wishful thinking; if Hitler had not become Reich chancellor, or been put on trial after the war, it almost goes without saying that things would have been better. A few works in this genre, notably the actor and comedian Stephen Fry's *Making History* (London, 1996), address the more profound question of exactly what was the balance of personal and impersonal historical factors in the rise and triumph of Nazism, concluding that things would have turned out in a similar manner anyway even if Hitler had not been around. Which you choose depends not only on how far you think great individuals steer the course of history, for good or evil, but also on how far you blame Hitler personally for the crimes of Nazism, or how far (like Fry) you pin the blame on the German people. Ultimately, as Fry's novel made clear, such fantasies are — like depictions of Hitler having survived the war — meant as much for entertainment as for anything else. Hitler belongs so vividly to the Nazi milieu, to the rallies and parades, speeches and propaganda, that it is intriguing to think of him living out a more or less conventional bourgeois existence in exile. Yet we know from a mass of evidence that Hitler did not actually want to survive defeat in war at all. At the core of his being, he believed in what he thought of as the Darwinian logic of the survival of the fittest and the struggle for existence of all against all, and if he failed, as he did, the only way out was through a sacrificial death, a belief shared by hundreds of other leading Nazis, including Goebbels, Goering, Himmler, and large numbers of generals, government ministers, and senior Nazi officials, who committed suicide at the end of the war in one of the greatest waves of self-immolation in history.[44]

Alternate histories have long been a staple of science fiction, so much so that since 1995 the World Science Fiction Convention has accorded public recognition to the genre in the announcement of two annual Sidewise Awards for Alternate History, which take their name from a 1934 short story "Sidewise in Time," by Murray Leister, in which parts of the earth change places with analogues from other timelines in 1935 so that a Roman legion from a timeline in which the Roman Empire survived into the modern age appears outside St. Louis, Missouri, the South wins the Civil War in some areas, and San Francisco is occupied by a victorious czarist Russia. The story is credited in the world of science fiction with effectively founding the modern genre of alternate-history stories, and indeed spawned a whole series of them in the following years. The boundaries between this world and the world of fictional alternate history on the one hand, and imaginary alternate history that claims to be fact on the other, are in some ways rather fluid.[45]

What distinguishes all this from more serious attempts at counterfactual history is the focus on causation common to the latter, which is usually absent from, or at least very subordinate in, the former. Counterfactual history foregrounds the effects of a single change in an existing causal chain, leading to a whole series of consequent changes in the course of history. Alternate history simply poses a world parallel to our own without enquiring too closely into how it came into being. Investigative medical or journalistic alternate history focuses on establishing that one single fact in history changed, devoting hundreds of pages to "proving" that Hitler survived in Argentina after the war, or that the "Rudolf Hess" in Spandau was someone else, but is not really interested in suggesting what difference these discoveries make to the course of history in a wider sense. The main interest in them, for both reader and writer, lies in the mechanics of the supposed proof itself.

Yet counterfactual history essentially belongs in the same world as these other, more obviously fictional works of the imagination, some of which have a much longer track record and came into fashion long before counterfactual histories became commonplace. Postmodern scepticism has freed up writers of all kinds to imagine what might have been and to tie their imaginings in one way or another to real historical events and real historical personages. In all of these various genres, the reader enters into an implicit pact with the author: both suspend their disbelief because they know how titillating it would be to imagine Hitler vegetating away in Argentina in 1964, or how politically persuasive it should be to meld the past with the present in imagining the British resisting incorporation into a Nazi-dominated Europe, or how morally regrettable it is that Hitler was not brought to justice after the war. To assess the usefulness or otherwise of counterfactuals in the study and interpretation of the real course of history, therefore, we have to put aside these more baroque products of the imagination, and try to pin down more precisely exactly how the counterfactual does relate to the real.

CHAPTER 4 *Possible Worlds*

Counterfactuals, or what some historians term counterfactuals, come in many different guises, and it is important to disentangle them before reaching a conclusion as to their usefulness or otherwise. Politically motivated fantasies, however widely they are believed, involving, for instance, the survival of Nazis in secret underground bunkers, conspiring to build an authoritarian New World Order, are not really counterfactual because they lack any real interest in cause and effect. Nor are minutely detailed pseudohistorical investigations purporting to show that Hitler did not die in the Berlin bunker, or escaped to Argentina: here the interest is in the alleged fact itself, not in its possible consequences. A more sinister alteration of the past can be seen in Stalin's attempt to airbrush his erstwhile rival Trotsky out of photographs taken during and immediately after the Bolshevik Revolution in Russia, and by Stalinist historians to write him out of the historical record — a practice chillingly represented in George Orwell's novel *1984*, where the hero Winston Smith's job is to rewrite old newspapers to delete evidence inconvenient to his political bosses in the present. Retrospective historical falsification of this kind is not really counterfactual, however, because it is merely concerned with rewriting the entire factual record, not with positing an alternative to it deriving from one small change in it. Nathaniel Hawthorne's story "P's Correspondence" falls into a similar, related category: he imagines a situation in which people like Napoleon, Shelley, or Byron have survived into the time at which he is writing — 1845 — instead of dying earlier, as they actually had.[1] This is simply imagining another reality, rather like Jonathan Swift's *Gulliver's Travels* or Thomas More's *Utopia* and other fictions of its kind. The survival of Hawthorne's subjects does not actually alter the larger situation of the world in 1845, it is simply interesting in itself, just as satirical alternative world like Brobdingnag or Lilliput do not actually change the real world their author lived in, they just hold up an ironic mirror to it.

Historical novels might seem to fall into the category of the counterfactual, and in his introduction to Sir John Squire's collection *If It Had Happened Otherwise* . . . , Sir John Wheeler-Bennett discusses what he called "imaginary history," including Anthony Trollope's and Benjamin Disraeli's parliamentary and political fictions. These are set in a recognizably contemporary or recent historical world—in their case, Victorian England—with recognizable institutions such as the House of Parliament, and recognizable figures, such as prime ministers and bishops, but narrate fictional events that never happened and depict fictional characters who never existed. The same might be said of many other novels in the genre begun by Sir Walter Scott's influential medieval fictions. But these are not counterfactual novels, because they do not posit any causal influence that created the parallel world they depict, as Wheeler-Bennett correctly noted. Moreover, neither they nor the much broader genre of historical novels make no significant changes to the basic historical context; they invent dialogue, character traits, and people, but not the big events, structures, or institutions of history; indeed, historical novelists usually go to considerable pains to "get it right" by reading and consulting standard historical works on their chosen period; Hilary Mantel's extraordinarily successful novels about the Tudor statesman and politician Thomas Cromwell, for example, have garnered numerous prizes and a vast readership not just because of the brilliance of their style, characterization, and structure, but also because of the patina of historical authenticity with which they decorate the action.[2]

Nor, for the same reason, can one classify as counterfactual the many novels written in England before the First World War warning of the consequences of continuing British complacency about the German arms buildup: novels in which Britain is invaded by German armies and ends up groaning under the iron heel of the Kaiser's jackboot, or similar fictions written in the 1930s, or the Eurosceptic novels of the 1990s like Andrew Roberts's *The Aachen Memorandum*, which envisions a future in which British domination by the EU in the twenty-first century is not dissimilar to what British domination by the Germans might have been like in the twentieth. Roberts's imaginary dystopian future is clearly based on a real dystopian past, but its conditional is based in the future and does not require any alteration to be made to what has happened already.[3] Similarly, novels or essays that reverse reality to provide the basis for a satirical commentary on the present, as, for example, with the imagined discovery and conquest of Europe by the Mayas or the Incas, the subject of fantasies by Spanish writers like Unamuno or Fuentes, do not depend on diverting the stream of time, but simply on turning reality upside down.[4] True counterfactual scenarios, whether historical or fictional, always involve drawing historical consequences, often far-reaching in nature, from altered *historical* causes.

A great deal of the time, what this produces is banal in the extreme. Jeremy Black's book, for example, is wholly devoted to accounts of how things might have turned out differently from the way they did, which, he claims repeatedly, all goes to show that contemporaries didn't know what was going to happen next, and therefore that they had considerable freedom of choice. Indeed, "rulers and ministers," he claims, had "the free will to enable them to defy the normative character of the policies that should derive from an understanding of national interests,"[5] or perhaps better said, their view of national interests was not necessarily the same as other people's. But the point here is that by bracketing out the factors that constrained their freedom of choice, we present a wholly false picture of that choice as having been unfettered. Rulers like Catherine the Great of Russia did indeed indulge in abrupt changes of policy, but always within the limits of what was acceptable; a good number of Russian czars were murdered because they transgressed those limits. To take a different example, namely, Ferguson's analysis of the outbreak of World War I, Aviezer Tucker notes that "Ferguson constructs decontextualized historical agents, isolated from larger cultural and economic contexts that precluded the kind of decision-making he would have undertaken" had he been a member of Asquith's government. Here again, to make the counterfactual work, individual decision makers have to be presented, implausibly, as free-floating agents. The larger contexts in which Sir Edward Grey actually made the decision to go to war in 1914 made it likely that even had the liberal government fallen as a result of the resignation of ministers who were against going to war with Germany, the British would have intervened in the war sooner or later anyway.[6]

Black's version of the "counterfactual," which amounts to no more than the *possibility* that things might have turned out differently, in no way helps us explain how or why they turned out as they did, not least because he prefers "counterfactuals that offer complexity and indeterminacy," rather than those that offer "answers." Ultimately, his counterfactuals are not really counterfactuals at all, or rather, they are not counterfactuals in the sense used by most other exponents of the genre. If the only thing that can be said in their favor is that they "make us much more aware of the role of the contingent," that is not very much, and once more confuses contingency with counterfactualism.[7] Other contributions to counterfactualist collections go in the opposite direction and eschew speculation altogether; thus, for example, Tucker points out that Michael Burleigh's archivally grounded essay in Ferguson's collection on Nazi plans for Europe is not counterfactual because it does not say what would have had to be different in the history of the war for them to have been put into effect.[8] A much larger category of writing speculates on too limited a level to be worth discussing as counterfactualism, namely, the very numerous essays of military history that discuss how a battle that went one way might have gone the other. Undoubtedly the most comprehensive of these is the volume published in 1997 by Dennis E. Showalter and Harold C. Deutsch, *If the Allies Had Fallen*. In no fewer than sixty separate essays, military historians consider counterfactuals ranging from what might have happened if the British had not managed to decode German radio traffic to "what if Stalin had adopted the supposed Shaposhnikov proposal for concentrating defenses along the Stalin line?" Many of these are unrealistic (e.g., what would have happened had Hitler let his generals get on with the job they were paid to do instead of interfering all the time). Essentially the essays, many of them very brief, are devoted to refighting the strategy and tactics of World War II with a view to rectifying the mistakes, or occasionally underlining the correct decisions, made by the participants.

Rather different in style and intent is another subcategory of counterfactual, extremely popular in Britain but also enjoying some vogue in the United States, namely, speculations about what would have happened had one or other politician become prime minister or president instead of the individual who actually did. The enterprising Conservative publisher Politico has made something of a minor industry out of such imaginings. Duncan Brack's 2006 collection *President Gore . . . and Other Things That Never Happened*, contains nineteen essays on individual politicians, mostly of the wishful thinking variety: Al Gore becomes U.S. president in November 2000 and avoids the Iraq War; the liberal statesman Gustav Stresemann does not die, as he did, in 1929 but lives on to save the Weimar Republic; Gavrilo Princip's bullet in Sarajevo misses the archduke Franz Ferdinand and the twentieth century turns out to be far less disastrous than it was in reality. More narrowly focused on British politicians, Duncan Brack and Iain Dale's 2003 collection *Prime Minister Portillo . . . and Other Things That Never Happened* contains a familiar mixture of wishful thinking and its reverse, peppered with not a few essays that conclude that things would have been much the same anyway had, for example, Ted Heath won the 1974 election or

Margaret Thatcher lost the 1979 election. Much the same can be said of the same editors' *Prime Minister Boris ... and Other Things That Never Happened* (London, 2011). All these collections are indeed counterfactuals, but they focus exclusively on individual personalities, taking what is known about them, perhaps spicing it up a bit, and then, acting in the belief that personality is all, they postulate (with a few exceptions) major changes resulting from the alteration in their personal fortunes. Slightly different is Francis Beckett's *The Prime Ministers Who Never Were* (London, 2011), which takes individual British politicians and puts them into Number 10 Downing Street. The usual suspects make their appearance, including Oswald Mosley, who creates the European Union, and Lord Halifax, who confounds his posthumous critics by deciding to carry on fighting Hitler. Reading through the often witty and irreverent pieces in all these collections, it is hard to avoid the conclusion that they are intended as a lighthearted entertainment for the chattering classes, perhaps also as an implicit encouragement to aspiring politicians.

For all their emphasis on the seriousness of their intentions, the new counterfactualists are not—fortunately for their readers— averse to mixing argument with entertainment or larding their speculations with whimsy and humor. Reviewers of the Roberts collection noted that all twelve essays were "good" and "entertaining" and praised their "playful" nature, calling the book "a hymn to the accidental and the erratic."[9] Humor creeps into even the most straight-faced counterfactuals, as for example when Holger Herwig has a collaborationist British government under the rule of the Germans appoint William Joyce ("Lord Haw-Haw") as director-general of the BBC.[10] Dominic Sandbrook's series of forty counterfactual historical essays written for the *New Statesman* in 2010–11 is clearly intended as an entertainment (the only really serious one, the last in the series, and some four times the length of any of the others, is predictive, focusing on the performance of David Cameron's Conservative-led coalition government in its first five years of office, from 2010 to 2015, even if it is written as a pseudohistorical article from the perspective of the end of this period). Sandbrook ranges across the whole of recorded history, beginning by having Egypt replace Rome after Octavian loses the Battle of Actium ("in the long term the rise of Egyptian power was inevitable") and Africans, convinced of Europeans' "stupidity, indolence and general inferiority," launching a "Scramble for Europe" in the fullness of time. William the Conqueror loses the Battle of Hastings, and the Anglo-Saxons continue in power up to the administration of "Chief Ealdorman Aedgifu Thatcher," maintaining a sturdy British independence from the Continent (a bit of Eurosceptic wishful thinking here, perhaps). Henry V of England lives into a ripe old age and conquers France (more wishful thinking), with Joan of Arc as his mistress (a likely story), but the united Anglo-French kingdom becomes too remote from the people, and the monarchy is overthrown when the Tower of London is stormed in 1789 by a republican mob led by Charles James Fox. Catholicism triumphs in England in two of Sandbrook's fantasies, to be led in the present by "Cardinal Dawkins," but the nation fails to industrialize and slips into a "nightmare: the civil war of the 1930s, the leftist massacres of priests and nuns, and the reactionary backlash under the long, ultra-clerical rule of President Muggeridge" (this is the very opposite of the wishful thinking usually characterized by those who imagine the failure of Protestantism in early modern England).[11]

This is all great fun, and Sandbrook's determination to keep it so is evidenced by his rigorous avoidance of topics that might get too serious, like a possible Nazi occupation of Britain. As he nears the present, his amusing counterfactuals focus more heavily on British politics, often achieving their effect through witty reversals of what we know happened, dexterous parallels with the present, and unexpected twists and turns in the imaginary story. One should not burden these brilliantly clever brief essays with a ponderous excess of analytical zeal. Still, it is noticeable that most of the time, Sandbrook offers not a counterfactual history, in the sense of one change in the chain of events leading on to a series of other changes that seem with at least some degree of plausibility to follow from it, but a parallel history in which, for example, Oliver Cromwell's son Richard ("Farmer Dick") does not retire to the country but becomes the Merry Monarch, to be succeeded in due course by "the dissolute George Cromwell in the 1820s" (i.e., a parallel George IV), a "tipsy, philandering Herbert Henry Cromwell" in the early 1900s (a parallel H. H. Asquith, the actual prime minister of the day), and even, in the primaries for the presidency founded in the seventeenth century by Oliver, "two Cromwells, Praise-God and Ed" (the Miliband brothers, who fought the Labour Party leadership in 2010, needless to say).[12]

In this lengthy series of short essays, Sandbrook is following the procedure set by Niall Ferguson in the afterword to his *Virtual History* volume, which posits an alternative history from 1646 to 1996, the date at which the book was completed. Ferguson has a great deal of fun attacking "determinists" who see the alternative course of history he describes as having been inevitable, presenting in his afterword what we know actually happened as a series of "counterfactuals" and thus repeatedly emphasizing the contingency of events. The narrative starts with the Royalists winning the English Civil War, and goes on to a future in which the Stuarts still become constitutional monarchs whose political flexibility and military skill allow the American colonies to be retained and the French Revolution to be avoided by financial reform; in addition, industrialization brings rising living standards that appease working-class discontent, Marx becomes a "millenarian Jewish prophet" and Lenin an Orthodox priest (later executed as a German spy), and the Holy Roman Empire is reformed through an Austro-Prussian alliance and keeps going as a decentralized federation through the nineteenth century, winning the First World War in 1915 while Britain stays neutral. The result is a "European Union" that respects the integrity of the British Empire, but still falls under the influence of the Nazis, who transform it into a "leader-state," conquer France and invade Britain, forcing it to join the new "German-European Union." In eastern Europe, the Germans defeat the Russians, but Hitler's death from the bomb planted by Stauffenberg destroys German morale, the Russians, led by the Patriarch Djugashvili (Stalin) counterattack, the Japanese bring the Americans into the war, but D-Day fails, and the Russians end up in control of Europe. In Britain, Prime Minister Thatcher loses the Falklands War and is succeeded by Michael Foot, whose calamitous premiership helps open the way to the economic and political collapse of the West and the breakup not only of the transatlantic confederation but also of the United Kingdom into its constituent parts. The way is open for the future dominance of the East.[13]

Cleverly weaving together the threads spun by the preceding essays in the book, this is a highly entertaining narrative that repeatedly brings a smile to the lips. Yet what is offered here runs counter to the general tenor of the *Virtual History* collection in a number of ways. First of all, it is patently intended as a *jeu d'esprit* in the style of Sir John Squire's collection (and as an entertainment it is a good deal superior). Ferguson's intention, as announced in his preface, is clearly to get away from this kind of thing and establish counterfactual history as a serious tool of scholarship.[14] Secondly, what the afterword offers is in fact not a counterfactual history, an altered event or circumstance leading through an apparently logical chain of consequences on to an altered state of affairs some time in the future, but, like Sandbrook's essays, a *parallel* history that shadows the history that actually happened but reverses it at every step. Causation is thrown out the window, and there is no attempt to consider how one change in the pattern of events might have affected others. It is simply asserted, for example, that a victory by Charles I in the seventeenth century would have led in time to a constitutional monarchy in Britain, though no reasons are given for supposing this would have happened. Ferguson has to do this so as to get history roughly back on course, as he has to have a First World

War and a Second World War; otherwise the narrative would drift too far away from the actual course of events and so cease to mirror them. But this procedure is entirely arbitrary and ignores both the possible chains of causation and the possible intervention of contingency.

In Ferguson's "virtual history," Argentina wins the Falklands War in 1982, for example. But the point of course is that had Charles I been victorious over the Parliamentarians in the seventeenth century, it is probable that the subsequent course of events over the next three centuries, though unpredictable, would have been such that there would have been no Falklands War, because an event such as the Falklands War is the product of a specific set of historical circumstances that in practice would not have occurred without a whole series of previous historical circumstances; a lengthy chain of causation, in other words. Indeed if Charles I had been victorious over the Parliamentarians, it is unlikely that Mrs. Thatcher would have been prime minister in Britain 340 years later, since the conditions that would have enabled women to achieve the vote, stand for Parliament, and lead political parties, might never have materialized. Altering one part of the kaleidoscope of history shakes up all the others in ways that are quite unpredictable. In this narrative, Ferguson jettisons all the rules and cautions he has so carefully elaborated earlier in the book and engages in wild historical fantasy.

Nor is this fantasy in any way value-neutral. A counterfactual narrative that includes the survival of the British Empire (including North America and ruled by the Stuarts), along with the Holy Roman Empire, into the late twentieth century, the absence of the French and Russian Revolutions, and more besides, is conservative wishful thinking with a vengeance. Yet although Aviezer Tucker claims that Ferguson develops these ideas in fulfillment of "some kind of personal utopia,"[15] there are negative elements too, notably the loss of the Falklands War, the disastrous premiership of Michael Foot, and the ominous rise of the East, serving as a warning for the future. Conservative Euroscepticism appears yet again in the portrait of the European Union as an expanded German Reich, though wishful thinking then has it destroyed in the end. Such imaginings go far beyond anything that is even remotely plausible; nor, it is clear, is it intended to be. Just to take a handful of examples: the victory of the Stuarts in the seventeenth century would have been unlikely to have led to a constitutional monarchy unless there were profounder social and economic forces at work. An absolutist Stuart England was hardly likely to have been the site of the industrial, political, scientific, technological, and indeed sociopolitical achievements that underpinned the imperial domination achieved by Britain in the nineteenth century.

A Europe dominated by the German military, as I have already suggested, would have been unlikely in 1915 to have allowed the British Empire to continue in its previous form, as indeed the much weaker Germany of the Kaiser was already contemplating in the decade and a half before his putative victory in the First World War. The historical record shows that Michael Foot invested just as much personal and political capital in the Falklands War as did Mrs. Thatcher, so that a defeat would have damaged him too (though one could also speculate that it would have won her a sympathy vote in the following election). Moreover, Ferguson's parallel narrative contradicts other counterfactual hypotheses he has developed elsewhere. In his own essay in the volume, for instance, he hypothesizes, as we have seen, that a German victory in the First World War would have prevented the spread of the bitter resentments and economic catastrophes that destroyed the Weimar Republic and brought Hitler to power, whereas in the afterword he has Hitler coming to power anyway. Even if we do not take the afterword too seriously, this is a contradiction that suggests a strong degree of arbitrariness in such speculations.

The suspicion of arbitrariness is underlined by counterfactual essays that offer alternative courses following the initial change of circumstance rather than trying to build up a coherent case for one particular chain of consequences. Thus, for example, in Roberts's collection the Catholic historian Antonia Fraser starts by presenting an "optimistic" scenario in which a successful Gunpowder Plot, having blown up king and Parliament in 1605, enthrones a new monarch, Elizabeth II (known to history as "the Winter Queen" through her short-lived occupancy of the Bohemian throne at the beginning of the Thirty Years' War in 1618 as wife of the quickly deposed Protestant Elector Palatine), reconciles Catholics and Protestants, establishes religious toleration, and cements a close alliance with France, all arguments of the "wishful thinking" variety. A "pessimistic" scenario, she says, however, conceding "an inexorable beat to the march of history," sees religious strife continuing.[16]

More strikingly still, quite a few counterfactual speculations end up by concluding that things would have taken the course they did anyway. In Ferguson's volume, John Adamson describes a victory for Charles I making little real difference in the end, given the strength of the forces working in favor of an increase in parliamentary power, thus implying that the Civil War and the execution of Charles I were historically unnecessary. Like Fraser's essay this embodies a strong element of wishful thinking but also admits that chance events only have a limited effect on the course of history, thus rather going against the editor's proclamation of the supremacy of contingency and chance in history.[17] Anne Somerset sees Philip II's conquest of England after a successful invasion by the Spanish Armada in 1588 as making little difference in the end: a reconversion to Catholicism does little harm, English autonomy is preserved, Parliament meets as before, and Shakespeare writes his great plays. Simon Sebag Montefiore has Stalin panicking when the Germans invaded in June 1941 and reached the gates of Moscow six months later. He flees the Soviet capital (in reality, after a great deal of hesitation, he decided to stay, though it was a close-run thing), and the Soviet forces then abandon the city. But Foreign Minister Molotov and the Politburo arrest and shoot Stalin, who is replaced by Molotov, the great general Marshal Zhukov mounts a successful counterattack, and the Red Army wins the war anyway. Molotov stays in power until his death in 1986, when Mikhail Gorbachev takes over and implements reforms that bring about the end of the Soviet Union. In other words, Stalin's abandonment of Moscow in December 1941 makes no difference in the long run. Similarly, in the scenario painted by Conrad Black, where the Japanese do not attack Pearl Harbor, the Americans still enter the war against the Axis powers; while Jonathan Haslam concludes that even had there not been an ideological confrontation between the Soviets and the West, the Cold War would have happened for geopolitical reasons in any case.[18]

The limited support many of these essays give in practice to the cause of counterfactuals as a vehicle for overcoming "determinism," in the sense of the prioritization of larger historical forces over smaller, personal, chance, and contingent events and circumstances, is compounded by the fact that despite Ferguson's criticisms of wishful thinking, other contributions to his volume, and a number of the contributions to Roberts's collection, and still others again, fall headlong into the trap of imagining things would have been better had they been different. In his contribution to Roberts's collection, the right-wing Anglo-Polish historian Adam Zamoyski envisions a world after Russia's defeat by Napoleon in 1812 in which there is no socialism and no nationalism to breed wars, and Russia is driven back to the margins of Europe and therefore not in a position to oppress Poland, as it did in reality for the whole of the nineteenth century and much of the twentieth; but Zamoyski is evenhanded enough to posit a future in which Europe, while prosperous and united in something that looks remarkably like the European Union, is hamstrung by a bureaucratic system that crushes economic and cultural initiative. The Eurosceptic wishful thinking so evident in Zamoyski's contribution comes in again as Norman Stone speculates that the putative failure of the assassination attempt on the archduke Franz Ferdinand at Sarajevo in 1914 would have been followed after a time by a violent implosion of the Ottoman Empire and its partition between Britain and Russia (thus involving the withdrawal of Russia from Europe and the strengthening of the British Empire). The Germans and French, who had missed the feast, join together in an economic federation looking, once more, like the present-day European Union, while Britain stands aside and prospers as a global power — another example of Eurosceptic counterfactual historical fantasy. Andrew Roberts has Lenin assassinated in 1917, the Bolsheviks taking a more moderate course than they did, the liberal Alexander Kerensky concluding peace, and a constitutional Russia helping defeat the Nazis in 1938, leading to the overthrow of Hitler and his Third Reich.[19] In all of this, wishful thinking trumps historical sense, and the extrapolation of consequences over the decades is too far-reaching to be convincing.

In Roberts's collection, the right-wing journalist Simon Heffer's essay on the consequences of the bomb set off at the Conservative Party conference in Brighton in 1984 has Prime Minister Thatcher killed in the blast (in fact, of course, she survived) and being succeeded by Michael Heseltine, a charismatic Tory but committed European. The essay falls into the mold of "there-but-for-the-grace-of God" as Heseltine divides his party with his pro-European policies and opens the door for Labour to win the 1992 election. But the damage would already have been done, and "Britain would have been set as a highly taxed, inefficient country like modern France, Germany or Japan." In similar vein, in a knockabout piece, David Frum imagines a U.S. president Gore hamstrung by environmentalist scruples, political correctness, and respect for international institutions when faced with the destruction of the Twin Towers in New York by Al-Qaeda in 2001, so that he is unable to mount an adequate response.[20] The possible objections to the politically driven imaginings here are legion. The evidence is that it was Mrs. Thatcher, with her late-onset Euroscepticism, who divided the Conservative Party, while Heffer's negative image of France, Germany, and Japan would not be recognized by many even in the 1990s. Similarly, the real victor of the U.S. presidential election of 2000, George W. Bush, turned out by common consent to be one of the most incompetent American presidents of the modern era, and his illegal and poorly thought-out invasions of Afghanistan and Iraq achieved very few concrete results in the end.

A large number of these essays ignore Ferguson's requirement that only alternatives actually consciously considered by contemporaries may be taken into account when developing a counterfactual. In practice, they throw a deus ex machina into the workings of history, whether it is a bomb that kills Margaret Thatcher, or an election that brings Al Gore to power, or a military victory by a general who was actually defeated, or some other reversal of historical circumstance that actually had little or nothing to do with alternatives confronting a decision maker. Grey in 1914, or Churchill and Halifax in 1940, may fulfill Ferguson's requirement, but very few of the historians who spin out their counterfactual scenarios follow suit, preferring to focus on other pieces of the historical mosaic. This is, of course, because the requirement to take a decision as the starting point proposes an impossibly narrow area in which counterfactuals can operate. But in practice that area is narrow enough anyway. Counterfactuals have almost always been hypothesized in the history of politics and policies, diplomacy, war, and government, and in these fields only in explanations of events.

Some advocates and practitioners of "counterfactual history" share this view, from Robert Cowley, seeking to use it to restore belief in great men, to Jeremy Black, who similarly concedes that the "undermining of any sense of necessity has tended to appeal largely to historians working on those aspects of history where contingent events and human actions are most intuitively central, such as political and military history."[21] It is striking how often the same topics turn up in the counterfactual world, from Charles Martel and the Spanish Armada to the Battle of Waterloo and the Second World War. Of the twelve essays in Andrew Roberts's collection, nine deal with wars, while the other three, respectively, ask what would have happened had the Gunpowder Plot succeeded, had Margaret Thatcher been killed by the Brighton bomb, or had Al Gore and not George W. Bush won the presidential election in 2002. Cowley's first collection is exclusively devoted to military history; and rare indeed are the contributions to the genre that stray beyond the realm of high politics and warfare, like William H. McNeill's essay on what would have happened had the potato not reached Europe, or Joel Mokyr and Kenneth Pomeranz's essays in *Unmaking the West* on alternative scenarios of economic history.[22]

For the vast majority of counterfactualists, as Tristram Hunt has pointed out, "'what-if' versions of the past posit the powerful individual at the heart of their histories: it is a story of what generals, presidents and revolutionaries did or did not do. The contribution of bureaucracies, ideas or social class is nothing to the personal fickleness of Josef Stalin or the constitution of Franz Ferdinand."[23] Yet, paradoxically, once the counterfactual narrative is launched, the personality at the center of the fantasy takes a back seat. The attention is all focused on the general, contextual factors that he or she affects by being killed (or not) or by taking a decision at odds with the one he or she actually took, or by winning (or losing) a battle or some similar action. Lubomir Dolezel, indeed, suggests that "historians focus on modulating significant (global) social, political, economic, or military historical conditions" in the counterfactual worlds they create, not on modulating the individual human being. "For counterfactual history, the individual is interesting only as a 'leader' of social, historically relevant actions or as an occasional agent of historically significant events."[24] When Napoleon wins the Battle of Waterloo, the world political order is changed; when the Gunpowder Plot succeeds, England becomes Catholic; Franz Ferdinand is not assassinated, so World War I would not have happened and the whole subsequent history of Europe and America would have been changed; when Britain stays out of the First World War, the European Union is created.

As these and many other examples suggest, counterfactualism focuses almost exclusively on traditional, old-fashioned political, military, and diplomatic history of the sort that used to be dominant in the 1950s. Even in *Unmaking the West* most of the contributions are on wars and revolutions. And indeed it more or less has to be so. Large-scale counterfactuals are implausible by their very nature. The leap, for example, from the absence of the Black Death in fourteenth-century France to a fall in fertility in the eighteenth century that led to an acceleration of economic growth, as proposed in Geoffrey Hawthorn's volume, is unsupported either by the extremely unlikely starting point, or by convincing historical linkages that posit a consequence over three hundred years later in the development of industry through a combination of labor shortage and high consumer demand such as happened in Britain.[25] Similarly, Joel Mokyr, in asking how science and technology might have developed if there had been no industrial revolution in the West, is compelled to admit that "at the end of the day, it is hard to know precisely whether oriental science, had it been left alone long enough by the West, would not have developed into something so radically different from what we are use to that we cannot even imagine it."[26] So this in itself is one major reason to be sceptical of the more far-reaching claims of counterfactual history: it not only assumes but also implicitly preaches a history where politics and warfare are the most important subjects to be studied; in other words, it advocates a narrow, traditional approach to the past that most historians have long since moved beyond, an area, however, where counterfactuals are almost impossible to deploy. Nowadays, the world's most innovative historians focus overwhelmingly on social, economic, and cultural history, on global and transnational representations of the past, not on political or diplomatic history.

When it comes to painting a larger picture that goes beyond the political or the military, indeed, Ferguson himself falls back into what looks very much like determinism. Thus in his book *Civilization*, Ferguson explains the fact that Europe dominated the world between 1815 and 1914 by arguing that European economies were based on competition, European science was superior to that of China and other civilizations, European law respected property rights and gave rise to stable forms of government, European medicine improved health and life expectancy, European society was based on consumer culture, and Europeans worked harder than anyone else. As he goes through these factors chapter by chapter, the unavoidable cumulative impression is one of inevitability. These were all long-term developments, beginning at the end of the Middle Ages if not before. By 1800 these factors were all in place, making European supremacy after 1815 inevitable. Alternative hypotheses—counterfactuals—do not come into this history, though according to Ferguson elsewhere they would undermine the determinism of this narrative.[27]

If even Ferguson implicitly concedes that counterfactuals are inappropriate when we are dealing with large-scale historical change, then how possible is it to devise procedures that avoid the many pitfalls that threaten the unwary practitioner who tries to apply them on a narrower front, from politically driven wishful thinking to implausible chains of consequences? Geoffrey Parker and Philip Tetlock have issued some basic rules of counterfactual history to the contributors to their volume of counterfactual essays, *Unmaking the West*. There has to be a "minimal-rewrite" rule, they say, along the lines suggested by Ferguson, to avoid arbitrariness. The ceteris paribus rule is another, or in other words, the rule that a counterfactual must only make one change in the causal chain and leave everything else the same as it was in reality. Thus, for example, as Aviezer Tucker points out, the counterfactual speculations of Jonathan Clark in Ferguson's volume—had there been no "Glorious Revolution" in 1688, America would have remained part of the British Empire—are meaningless because the change in the initial condition ignores the ceteris paribus rule; that is, it is too large to make the speculation historically sustainable, for England would have needed to have been a completely different society and polity for there to have been no "Glorious

Revolution" overthrowing the Catholic absolutist James II and bringing in the Protestant Dutch monarch William III.[28]

A self-denying ordinance whereby counterfactual scenarios do not extrapolate themselves too far into the future is the second principle suggested by Parker and Tetlock, and in doing so they add to Clark's destructive point about the implausibility of very long-term scenarios by noting that "the deeper authors try to see into the futures of their counterfactual worlds, the frailer their connecting principles become."[29] Finally, in order to get round Carr's charge, exemplified by so many contributions to other collections of counterfactual essays, that such speculations are hopelessly self-serving, Parker and Tetlock asked their contributors to be explicit about their perspective and allow themselves to be self-critical, as all historians should be. The acid test of essays written in this frame of mind is surely whether they contribute anything to historical knowledge or understanding. Surveying the contributions to their volume at the end, the editors make the point that "close-call" counterfactuals that show how a crucial decision or event might easily have gone another way can contribute usefully to a sense of the possibilities open to contemporaries. But this is not quite the point. The real interest of close-call counterfactuals is in pointing up the *limited nature* of such possibilities and the *constraints* within which they operated.

In writing about the Nazi seizure of power, for example, I argued in my book *The Coming of the Third Reich* that the choices facing Germany in 1933 were essentially between an authoritarian military regime and a Nazi dictatorship. It is certainly true, as Parker and Tetlock say, taking their cue from empirical studies by Henry Turner, that the Nazis were in decline, in voting support, financial resources, and internal cohesion, at the end of 1932 and the beginning of 1933, and that if you follow the many twists and turns of the complex political negotiations that brought Hitler into the chancellorship on 30 January 1933, chance played a role. But we do not need a counterfactual to tell us that, and indeed Parker and Tetlock do not deploy one. Moreover, to focus exclusively on the small number of decision makers around President Hindenburg, whose maneuverings made Hitler chancellor, while inevitably underlining the impact of chance factors such as "personal affinities and aversions, injured feelings, soured friendships, and desire for revenge,"[30] is to bracket out the larger picture of rapidly growing, mass, murderous Nazi violence on the streets, combined with the complete ungovernability of the Reichstag, which dissolved in chaos, with Communists and Nazis chanting slogans at each other across the chamber and joining together only to vote down any measure proposed by the government. This was an intolerable situation that could not be sustained, least of all in a massive economic crisis that left well over a third of the population unemployed and bankruptcies and bank failures across the land. The political crisis could only be resolved by bringing the Nazis into government in one form or another. The key factor was not so much the political decline of the Nazis from the elections of July 1932 to the elections of November 1932, though this, fatally, helped persuade the conservatives around Papen and Hindenburg that they could control them, but the Nazi storm troopers' escalating use of violence, which, the army leader General Schleicher feared, was pushing the country into civil war.[31]

The whole history of Germany from the fall of the last democratic government in 1930 had narrowed the options down and eliminated the possibility of the return of democracy. This at least is what key contemporaries thought. One might speculate that more skillful maneuvering by men like General Schleicher might have brought a representative of the army to power in Germany instead of the Nazis, though the Nazis would either have had to be put down by force — a difficult proposition, given the fact that the storm troopers were far more numerous than the army's own soldiers — or still brought into some kind of coalition. Even had this happened, it is reasonable to suppose that, given the policies of the army officer corps and its commitment to reversing the Treaty of Versailles, rearming the nation, remilitarizing the

Rhineland, invading Austria and Czechoslovakia, and in general preparing to reverse the defeat of 1918, would have at least brought a general European war much closer, especially since they would have needed to keep the Nazis onside. In practice, indeed, a coalition government was formed, bringing together the Nazis, the conservatives, and the army. Hitler comprehensively outmaneuvered his coalition partners and established a one-party dictatorship in a few months. The dynamism of the Nazis, their violence on the streets, the ruthless ambition of their leader — all these speak in favor of such a hypothesis.[32]

The way in which these scenarios contribute to historical understanding is by making it clear that the immediate restoration of Weimar democracy and the maintenance of the international status quo in Europe was not an option in 1932–33. The point is to argue not for the freedom of maneuver that German politicians had in 1933, but for the lack of it. Similarly, the experience of the uprising of the Austrian Socialists against the dictatorship of Dollfuss in February 1934, gunned down by the army in a few days, can show that even had the Communists and Social Democrats been united in Germany, they would not have been able to withstand the violence of the German armed forces, or the Nazis, let alone both. The aim here is to undermine any kind of wishful thinking on these counts, or, in other words, to reinforce the depiction of actual historical reality in the narrative of events in Germany in 1932–33, not primarily to emphasize the openness of the future at this crucial point; it was open only in the most limited sense. Such speculations fit in well enough with Parker and Tetlock's criteria of "minimal rewrite" or of "close-call" or short-term speculation on possible alternatives, though not with the purposes for which they think they should be undertaken, but in the end, they scarcely fit the description of "counterfactual" in the way it is usually applied.

In another area, Parker and Tetlock criticize the claim that Kaiser Wilhelm II was unaware of the precariousness of Bismarck's achievement of German unity and saw the process as historically preordained. "The only way to argue [t]his case," they claim, "is by making a host of counterfactual assumptions about how easy or difficult it is to reroute European history in the mid-nineteenth century." But this is not true at all; in fact the case can easily enough be made by quoting Bismarck, the Kaiser, and their contemporaries on the topic. The fact is that Bismarck thought that Germany's position in Europe and the world was precarious, the Kaiser did not, and both modeled their behavior as statesmen on these beliefs. A simple factual narrative of German unification, so long as it doesn't fall victim to the inevitabilism of the Borussian school of historians, indeed a simple factual narrative of the Battle of Sadowa, should be enough without any explicit counterfactual speculations to demonstrate the role of chance in the process, but then of course the Kaiser did indeed think victory at Sadowa was preordained, as it was in Sedan. The crucial point here is what the two men thought; the historian does not need to decide whether they were right in order to understand their actions, though the Kaiser did indeed in the end risk everything Bismarck had achieved and brought his empire to ruin in the First World War. To reach such a conclusion is not to claim one knows better than contemporaries what they should have done; it's simply a matter of historical observation.

Finally, Parker and Tetlock argue that what they call reversionary counterfactualism, emphasizing not short-term chance events but longer-term large-scale processes, can be helpful in explaining, for instance, how and why things such as industrialization or changes in the balance of power between nations and states happened the way they did; that is, the counterfactual speculation leads back in the end to the conclusion that things would have been the same even had events and processes occurred rather differently. It is possible to imagine for instance, Hitler winning the war against the Soviet Union only to be destroyed by the American atom bomb, so Germany lost the war in the end anyway. The argument here is that such thought-experiments help weigh up the importance of different, impersonal factors in historical outcomes. But the problem here is that one can just as easily do this without such thought-experiments. They also seem to violate Parker and Tetlock's principle of avoiding long-term rewrites of history. And anyway, Nazi Germany was defeated without the intervention of the atom bomb, so what is the point of imagining that it might have needed the bomb to achieve this?

Parker and Tetlock's distinction between short-term and long-term counterfactualism is very similar to that made by Allan Megill between what he calls *restrained* counterfactual history, which "involves an explicit canvassing of alternative possibilities that existed in a real past," and *exuberant* counterfactual history, or "virtual history," which "deals in past historical outcomes that never in fact came to be."[33] *Restrained* counterfactual history is restrained because it starts out from an actual event and looks back in time, moving "from observed effect to hypothesized cause." Thus, for example, John Adamson's essay "England without Cromwell: What If Charles I Had Avoided the Civil War?," in Ferguson's *Virtual History*, looks at a range of possible alternatives to what actually happened (namely, that Charles I fought and lost a civil war between 1640 and 1649 and was executed at the end, being replaced by Oliver Cromwell, the leading general on the opposing side, as "Lord Protector"), and devotes the bulk of his essay to explaining why these alternatives did not come to pass. This kind of counterfactual history is epistemologically relatively tenable, according to Megill, because it starts with known evidence and uses counterfactual speculation to argue about why things ended as they did and not differently. Indeed, Megill argues that *all* causal explanations in history must be counterfactual in this sense, because *all* causal explanations involve not only explaining why things turned out the way we know they did, but also why they did not turn out some other way.[34] For example, in explaining why Hitler came to power in 1933, we are also explaining why the German army did not come to power, why the Left failed to resist the Nazis, and why democracy was not restored.

Megill argues that historians need counterfactuals because they cannot, as a matter of principle, adduce regularities or constant conjunctions of repeated structures or larger influences as causes. We might say for example that imperialism caused the First World War, but we cannot say that imperialism causes all wars. In practice, saying that imperialism caused the First World War is a perfectly reasonable statement, even if it operates at a very high level of generalization (it does not of course say why the war broke out when it did, or why some countries fought on one side and some on the other). And of course it has an implied counterfactual, or, in this sense, an alternative vision of what might have happened: if there had been no imperialism, there would have been no First World War. But this is not the main point of the argument: it is not necessary in any way to discuss what would have happened in 1914 had there been no imperialism, so there is no need for counterfactual speculation. Historians, then, only need counterfactuals at a much lower level of generality, following Parker and Tetlock's principle of the minimal rewrite. *Exuberant* counterfactual history, argues Megill, operates not from an actual event back to a hypothesized cause, but from an invisible or hypothesized cause to an event or sequence of events that never actually took place. In other words, "speculations concerning virtual history are far more deeply permeated by under-supported assumptions about the real nature of the world than is the case when the normal canons of historical method operate." These speculations amount in effect to a theory that drives the counterfactual speculations, because they lack any direct evidence to support them.[35] Thus the argument here becomes metaphysical rather than historical.

Aviezer Tucker has put these same points in a slightly different way. Tucker points out that "every counterfactual has a *ceteris paribus* clause: the historian assumes that the historical reality remained constant, except for the examined factors."[36] So, for example, if we thought about what might have happened had Hitler been killed in the First World War (a far from unlikely contingency), we would assume everything else remained the same, in order to make the speculation meaningful: Germany would lose the war, and the Nazi Party would still be created, only with a different leader; then we imagine what difference Hitler's absence might have made to its policies, its electoral prospects, and so on. Counterfactuals in other words have to be consistent with other things we know about the subject of the speculation: we change one thing but leave everything else the same. It would make little sense to speculate on the course events might have taken if the Nazi Party had been philosemitic because we know that far-right parties in Germany immediately after the First World War were antisemitic. The implication here is that to be meaningful at all, counterfactuals have to posit small changes not large ones. If we shake up the kaleidoscope of history by moving one piece then we can think creatively about the effect this might have on all the other pieces; but if we shake them all up, we can't make any generalizations at all. Nevertheless, who is to say that had Hitler been killed in the war, the Nazi Party would ever have come into existence after it, as opposed to the very ordinary fringe movement, the German Workers' Party, from which it emerged? The ceteris paribus rule leads to unconvincing decisions to ignore the possible effects of a changed starting point on later developments that the counterfactualist does not want to consider. Other things won't necessarily remain the same, in other words, and even this principle still leaves out the possibility of unforeseen chances.[37]

As Johannes Bulhof points out, many if not most historical investigations contain what he calls *modal* claims, by which he means that if *a* had not happened, then *b* would not have happened either. Counterfactuals in this sense permeate historiography because historians are concerned to explain why things happened, and this necessarily involves explaining why other things, alternatives, did not happen. But this is a truism. The crucial step that turns an absent but plausible alternative into a counterfactual is the extrapolation from it of further unrealized but plausible consequences. And in practice these are not central to the task of explaining why things happened as when and why they did. Thus, for example, Daniel Goldhagen's book *Hitler's Willing Executioners* argues that non-Germans such as the Ukrainian auxiliaries who manned the death camps of the Reinhard Action "were not essential to the perpetration of the Holocaust," and backs this with a counterfactual: "To be sure, had the Germans not found European (especially East European) helpers, then the Holocaust would have unfolded somewhat differently, and the Germans would likely not have succeeded in killing as many Jews." But this speculation—expressed in vague terms, as a possibility or at most a probability—is not actually necessary to the explanation, which is contained in Goldhagen's evidence-based statement that non-Germans were not essential to the Holocaust because "they did not supply the drive and initiative that pushed it forward." Naturally this supposes another counterfactual, namely, that if the Germans had not acted as they did, there would have been no Holocaust. But this is completely redundant as a statement, because we know from an enormous mass of evidence that the Germans did indeed originate, initiate, and implement the Holocaust and that Ukrainians and others were only auxiliaries.[38] All causal statements may indeed have implied alternatives, but it is not necessary to consider these alternatives and their implications in order to drive the causal explanation forward.

Bunzl argues that "the problem of the basis for deeming counterfactual judgments to be reliable is a function of the reliability of our claims on which we base the counterfactual judgments. If we base a counterfactual judgment on a causal claim, then the question is, how reliable is that causal claim?"[39] Thus, for example, it seems at first sight to be a reasonable statement that had partisans in Nazi-occupied Eastern Europe had nuclear weapons at their disposal they would have defeated Hitler's army, but the background condition here is implausible because if they had had nuclear weapons then other, richer, better resourced organizations would surely have got there before them, including the Nazis, but above all the Americans, so the entire background situation would have been entirely different. Thus, as Bunzl concludes, "a counterfactual inference is only as good as the assumptions that one makes about the background conditions."[40] Counterfactuals, however, can involve not only extrapolating forward in time from an alternative event to the one that actually happened, but also extrapolating back in time to see whether the same event would have occurred under different conditions or with changes in the antecedents. Counterfactuals in this sense are compatible with determinism because "some of the most interesting historical questions have to do with probing the stability of an outcome under a range of variations from the way things were."[41]

But this is only true, as many critics of "exuberant" or "long-range" counterfactualism have pointed out, if we stick as closely as possible to what was known, and use counterfactual speculation to understand why things turned out as they did. Understanding what the options and possibilities were helps us penetrate to the core of why one and only one became reality. For example, it helps understand the motives and purposes of the men who tried to kill Hitler on 20 July 1944 if we think about what might have happened had they succeeded. In practice, they enjoyed only very limited support among the armed forces, and the death of Hitler would probably have unleashed civil war as the SS and other fanatical Nazi troops fought to put them down and exact revenge. The plotters more or less knew this, and their final letters indicate they had moved on from thinking they could take over Germany and make peace with the Allies (unrealistic in the extreme, given the Allied policy of unconditional surrender) to rescuing at least an element of German honor by an act they knew to be in all probability self-sacrificial. Given their hostility to parliamentarism and their belief in social and political inequality, they were not likely to follow Hitler's death by trying to create a new, democratic Germany. Speculations such as these help identify what their real options were in July 1944, not least because they are based closely on evidence of what the plotters thought these options were.

It is altogether a different matter to extrapolate from this, as C. J. Sansom does, to a scenario in which the war on the Eastern Front in Europe continues as a result of a German victory over Britain, and a military plot to seize power succeeds in 1952 because an unwinnable war has continued for eight more years with massive loss of life, and — crucially — Hitler has died, freeing the military from their oath of allegiance to him.[42] There are plenty of risky conditionals here. Given the extent to which the Third Reich was outnumbered in human resources by the Soviet Union and outpaced by its production of arms, ammunition, and equipment by 1944, it is not at all certain that it could have continued fighting for a further eight years, and improbable that — as others have speculated — that the two powers were sufficiently evenly matched to fight each other to a standstill or a stalemate.[43] Still, the death or incapacity of Hitler would indeed, as many authors, from Philip K. Dick onward, have suggested, surely have unleashed a power struggle within the Nazi elite: and such was the centrality of Hitler to the whole Nazi system that it would have been unable to continue for much longer anyway, whether or not the military staged another revolt. German war graves commonly honored the dead as "fallen for *Führer* and Fatherland," and no other Nazi leader, neither Goering, nor Goebbels, wielded the same charisma as Hitler.

Historical explanation generally involves a concept of historical necessity — in other words, necessary causes — in which converging causal chains lead to a certain type of result without determining the particular form it takes. Thus, for example, we may say that the initial condition of Hitler's intention to wage a European war to establish German hegemony in Europe provided a necessary cause of the Second World War, but does not in itself explain why that war broke out in September 1939. For that to happen, other causal chains had to be set in motion — for example, the appeasement policy of Britain and France in the mid-1930s and its reversal in 1939, the successes of German rearmament, and so on; and there were also contingent events that influenced the outcome, such as the illness that made Hitler accelerate the drive to war because he was afraid he might die before being able to put into effect his original intention of starting a war in 1942. In this kind of analysis, according to Tucker, counterfactuals might be useful in understanding just how contingent a given event might have been.[44] Thus we cannot and should not imagine that Hitler had no intention at all of waging a general European war — that was the mistake the appeasers made — nor does it make sense to imagine Hitler would not have marched into Prague in March 1939, which was the event that brought appeasement to an end. But we can imagine what might have happened had the generals succeeded in their tentative plot to overthrow Hitler in 1938 because they did not think Germany was ready for war, or had Neville Chamberlain not secured the Munich agreement that made them abandon their plans, or had Hitler not decided to accelerate his external and internal aggression in 1937–38, and indeed in examining these events, we implicitly do engage in such speculations because these were contingencies that might easily have ended in different outcomes.

In the counterfactual scenarios that I have examined in detail, what is most striking perhaps are the radical divergences of opinion between the counterfactualists on the same topic, depending partly on their political motives, partly on the contemporary context within which they are writing. If Britain had signed a separate peace with Nazi Germany in 1940 or 1941, would Hitler have beaten the Soviet Union in the war on the Eastern Front, or would the two totalitarian powers have fought each other to a stalemate? Or, as Andrew Roberts speculated in 2001, contradicting his earlier views on the topic, would Stalin have conquered the whole of Europe, with horrendous consequences?[45] Would British institutions including the empire have been preserved, or would Hitler have imposed his will gradually on the British,

Nazifying their institutions, forcing them to surrender British Jews to be taken to Auschwitz, and dismantling their imperial possessions one by one? If Nazi Germany had occupied Britain would there have been mass collaboration or mass resistance? Would the Duke of Windsor have become a pro-Nazi puppet king or not? Would a collaborationist Number 10 Downing Street have been occupied by Lloyd George, Sir Oswald Mosley, Lord Halifax, Sir Samuel Hoare, or Rab Butler (Holger Herwig hedges his bets by having a collaborationist government under Edward VIII led by Halifax, Hoare, and Lloyd George, all three together)?[46] What, in any case, do these speculations tell us about the state of British and European politics in the 1930s and 1940s that we did not know already?

Such considerations apply to many if not most other counterfactuals as well. Surveying the contributions to their own collection of counterfactual essays, Parker and Tetlock point out that for Jack Goldstone, discussing English history in the late seventeenth century, "the exact moment of William III's death possesses great significance because he believes it would have unleashed a totally different and irreversible course for British, European, and even global history," while another of them, criticizing Goldstone's long-range extrapolation of this singular event, "believes it scarcely matters because William would have been succeeded first, by his wife Mary and, if she had predeceased William, by her sister Anne (as happened in 1702)."[47] The issue at hand here is one of the most oft-addressed in history counterfactuals, covered already in very different ways by Chesterton, Fraser, Russell, and many others: What would have happened had England been a Catholic country rather than a Protestant one? While Fraser and Chesterton, as Catholic historians, both think things would have been better (though as we have seen, Fraser concedes that they might not), Goldstone takes a far gloomier view. If William of Orange's invasion of England in 1688 had failed, he says, there would have been no scientific revolution, no parliamentary constitution, no British Empire, no modern world. As Carla Gardina Pestana has pointed out, this would have required James II, whom William in reality ousted in 1688, to have reached "a level of political sagacity rarely reached by any mere mortal, much less any Stuart king."[48] The power of James II to repress opposition in the country, which was massive by that time, would have had to be far greater than it actually was, while Protestantism would have needed to be far weaker. The English would not have accepted the status of a satellite of Louis XIV's France. The civil wars of a few decades before might well have begun all over again.

In terms of methodology, Pestana is "uncomfortable with the way in which Goldstone privileges certain kinds of causal explanations in his counterfactual," namely, the actions, beliefs, and character of great men. Similarly, Goldstone has James II destroying the scientific revolution by getting rid of Isaac Newton; yet of course we know that scientific breakthroughs in the seventeenth century involved far wider circles of men and a far more widespread field of knowledge. Goldstone might adhere in terms of events to the minimal-rewrite rule, which, as Pestana comments, is often put into effect "by finding someone to kill,"[49] but then has to ignore the ceteris paribus rule (by making James II an effective monarch, for example) in order to get his counterfactual to work. Moreover, one might point out in any case that some European countries were quite content to have a monarch of one religious denomination ruling over a population with another, and that there was no necessary opposition between Catholic belief and scientific enterprise, as the case of the Emperor Rudolf II and his patronage of scientists and astronomers such as Tycho Brahe and Johannes Kepler showed.[50]

All of this goes to show how counterfactual speculations frequently, perhaps even generally, tread on thin evidential ice, too often selecting the conditions of their starting point with insufficient care, and failing to distinguish between different levels of causation. They frequently tackle historical topics of enormous complexity, cutting the Gordian knot of interpretation by simply asserting the power of the individual actor to change things. Moreover, every counterfactual is locked into a particular historical interpretation that is almost bound in itself to be hugely controversial even before the initial change in the timeline is effected. Thus, for example, there have been many counterfactual essays about the outbreak of World War I — characteristically for the genre, they have focused either on the non-assassination of Franz Ferdinand or on the decision of the British foreign secretary not to go to war, rather than, say, on alternative outcomes of the decision-making process in the Russian, Habsburg, Serb, or other governments. Thus any counterfactual based on the outbreak of the war has to take into account the fact that there were multiple lines of causation intersecting in a whole variety of nonpredictable ways. They had already almost joined up in the winter of 1912–13 over war in the Balkans; it is likely they would have joined up in a different way at a different time had Franz Ferdinand not been shot, though one can never be quite sure. The variables are just too many for it to be plausible to isolate one and reduce the whole complex mess of causation to the effects of a single change in the causative chain.[51]

I have argued in this book that long-range counterfactual speculations are unconvincing and unnecessary for the historian because they elide too many links in the proposed causative chain after the initial altered event. As Eric Hobsbawm puts it, all that you can say if a condition is altered in a timeline, such as, for example, Lenin being stuck in Switzerland in 1917 instead of being able to make his way to Russia, is that "'things could have been very different' or 'not very different.' And you can't get any further, except into fiction."[52] Of course, counterfactualists do habitually say more, and this quickly leads them into trouble. Too often they fall prey to wishful thinking. Counterfactualists who propose sensible limitations to their thought experiments too often forget them altogether in the heady excitement of speculative imagining. Ferguson lays down some sane and workable rules about counterfactuals then breaks them in a whole variety of ways, whether by taking his speculations too far up the stream of time, or by descending into a morass of politically motivated wishful thinking. Parker and his colleagues insist on short-term counterfactuals based on minimal rewriting of the factual situation from which they start out, and then include long-term and large-scale discussions of vast imaginary social and economic changes extending over several centuries. Roberts wants to free his contributors from the tyranny of hindsight and open up history to contingency and chance but ends up including in his collection several essays that conclude that what happened was more or less inevitable anyway. Everyone in recent years has insisted on the seriousness of the counterfactual enterprise, but this doesn't stop many of them penning witty and whimsical essays designed as much to entertain as to inform, if not more so.

Wrestling with problems such as these, the German-born American historian Holger Herwig confessed that in considering what might have happened had Hitler won the war in the east, "a bewildering choice of possible counterfactuals confused me. Which to choose?"[53] In practice, the choice is the outcome of the historian's intention, political orientation, factual knowledge, and contemporary context. It also reflects to a degree the aesthetic purposes of the author, striving to produce the most satisfying, the most coherent and, often, the most entertaining counterfactual scenario. Based on a minimal rewrite, and confined to the short run, a counterfactual can illuminate the choices that confronted individual politicians and statesmen, and the limitations that the historical context imposed on those choices. But the further away it gets from the starting point the less useful it becomes, and the more it enters the worlds of alternative reality to which increasing numbers of people are turning in search of spaces for their imaginations to roam free, unfettered by facts. Frustration at the complexities and uncertainties of modern life leads them to inhabit the Middle Earth of Tolkien's *Lord of the Rings* rather than the Middle Ages of real historical time, or the rational world of Sherlock Holmes's Victorian London rather than the conditionally complex world of the late Victorian city. Such fantasy worlds are particularly appealing in times of political and cultural anxiety, uncertainty, crisis, or disappointment.[54] Far from demonstrating "how central counterfactual framing should be to serious historical research," as Parker and Tetlock have claimed,[55] I hope I have shown that it is not central at all, but marginal. It can be useful under certain strictly limited conditions and with strictly limited purposes, but surveying what is by now a very voluminous literature with hundreds of case studies in print, the conclusion surely has to be that it is most useful, and most interesting, as a phenomenon in itself, as a part of modern and contemporary intellectual and political history, worthy of study in its own right, but of little real use in the serious study of the past. As Max Weber observed: "In every line of every historical book, judgments of possibilities are hidden and must be hidden, if the publication is to have any intellectual value."[56]

Such a conclusion has been reached by a number of students of counterfactualism from the historian Gavriel Rosenfeld, who views counterfactualism's motives as "fundamentally presentist,"[57] to the literary scholar Benjamin Wurgaft, who points out that "the effort to ask such questions often serves as an excellent guide to the prejudices and interests of the historian asking them."[58] This is not least because, as Nietzsche remarked, the question "what would have happened if . . . ?" "turns everything into a matter of irony."[59] Counterfactuals are ironical because, ultimately, they always cast more light on the present than on the past. In the end, perhaps, the last word should be left to Walther Rathenau, himself, as we have seen, the subject of one of the more elaborate of counterfactual novels, by his Italian admirer Guido Morselli. Looking back in 1918 over the events of the First World War, and looking forward to the new world he hoped to make when peace came, Rathenau remarked: "History does not conjugate in conditionals, it speaks of what is and what was, not what would be and what would have been."[60]

NOTES

1. WISHFUL THINKING

1   Victor Hugo, *Les Misérables*, trans. Norman Denny (London, 1988 [1862]), pp. 279–324.

2   James Joyce, *Ulysses*, ed. Hans Walter Gabler (London, 1986 [1922]), p. 21.

3   "Le nez de Cléopatre: s'il eût été plus court, toute la face de la terre aurait changé," in Blaise Pascal, *Pensées*, ed. Léon Brunschwig (Paris, 1976), p. 71; Edward Hallett Carr, *What Is History?* 40th anniv. ed. (London, 2001 [1961]), pp. 91–93.

4   *The Adventures of Robert Chevalier, call'd De Beauchene, Captain of a Privateer in New-France* (London, 1745 [1732]).

5   Edward Gibbon, *The History of the Decline and Fall of the Roman Empire* (London, 1910 [1772–89]), vol. 5, p. 399; for Gibbon's Oxford experience, see his *Autobiography of Edward Gibbon, as originally edited by Lord Sheffield* (London, 1907 [1796]), pp. 31–55.

6   Isaac D'Israeli, "Of a History of Events Which Have Not Happened," in *Curiosities of Literature* (Paris, 1835), vol. 2, pp. 369–78. D'Israeli originally published the *Curiosities* in 1791, with a second volume in 1793, followed by various new editions, including one with a third volume in 1817, adding extra essays as he went along. For Alexander, see Livy, *Ab urbe condita*, book 9, sections 17–19; for *Tirant lo Blanc*, see the translation by David Rosenthal (London, 1984), pp. 555–624.

7   Christoph Rodiek, *Erfundene Vergangenheit: Kontrafaktische Geschichtsdarstellung (Uchronie) in der Literatur*, Analecta Romana 57 (Frankfurt am Main, 1997), p. 63.

8   Jean Tulard, ed., *Napoléon à Sainte-Hélène: Par les quatre évangélistes Las Cases, Montolon, Gourgaud, Bertrand* (Paris, 1981), pp. 326–7, quoted in Rodiek, *Erfundene Vergangenheit*, p. 67 (my

translation). See also Kai Brodersen, *Virtuelle Antike: Wendepunkte der Alten Geschichte* (Darmstadt, 2000).

9   Louis Geoffroy, *Napoléon apocryphe, 1812–1832: Histoire de la conquête du monde et de la monarchie universelle* (Paris, 1844 [1836]); Rodiek, *Erfundene Vergangenheit*, pp. 67–89.

10   Rodiek, *Erfundene Vergangenheit*, p. 72 n. 10; Emmanuel Carrère, *Le détroit de Behring: Introduction à l'uchronie: Essai* (Paris, 1986), pp. 18–32. Josephine actually died in 1814.

11   Rodiek, *Erfundene Vergangenheit*, pp. 67–76; see also Pierre Veber, *Seconde vie de Napoléon Ier* (Paris, 1924), and Louis Millanvoy, *Seconde vie de Napoléon (1821–1836)* (Paris, 1913).

12   Charles Renouvier, *Uchronie (L'utopie dans l'histoire): Esquisse historique apocryphe du développement de la civilisation européenne tel qu'il n'a pas été, tel qu'il aurait pu être* (Paris, 1876, reprinting articles in *Revue philosophique et religieuse* 7 (1857), pp. 187–208, and 510–41; and 8 (1857), pp. 246–79; see also Rodiek, *Erfundene Vergangenheit*, pp. 77–89, and Carrère, *Le détroit de Behring*, pp. 53–62. See more generally Paul Alkon, *Origins of French Fantastic Fiction* (Atlanta, GA, 1987).

13   Rodiek, *Erfundene Vergangenheit*, p. 79.

14   Ibid., *Erfundene Vergangenheit*, pp. 77–90. Renouvier's appendices fill more than a hundred pages of his book.

15   "If Napoleon Had Won the Battle of Waterloo," in George Macaulay Trevelyan, *Clio: A Muse, and Other Essays, Literary and Pedestrian* (London, 1913), pp. 184–200; reprinted in John Collings Squire, ed., *If It Had Happened Otherwise* (London, 1972 [1932]), pp. 299–312.

16   See David Cannadine, *G. M. Trevelyan: A Life in History* (London, 1992).

17   Edmund Blunden, "Sir John Collings Squire," rev. Clare L. Taylor, *Oxford Dictionary of National Biography* (Oxford, 2004), Index number 101036227.

18   See also the reworking of this fantasy in Geoffrey Hawthorn, *Plausible Worlds: Possibility and Understanding in History and the Social Sciences* (Cambridge, 1991), pp. 1–3.

19   Squire, *If It Had Happened Otherwise*, p. 48.

20   Arnold J. Toynbee, *A Study of History* (Oxford, 1934), vol. 2, *The Genesis of Civilisations*, part 2.

21   A Confederate victory in the Civil War is one of the most popular counterfactuals, though the consequences drawn differ very widely indeed. See Phil Patton, "Lee Defeats Grant," *American Heritage* 50 (September 1999), pp. 39–45.

22   William L. Shirer, "If Hitler Had Won World War II," *Look* (19 December 1961), pp. 28 and 43. See also the discussion in Gavriel Rosenfeld, *The World Hitler Never Made: Alternate History and the Memory of Nazism* (Cambridge, 2011), pp. 103–4. For speculative fiction imagining a Catholic England and a traditionalist papacy enduring to the late twentieth century, see Kingsley Amis, *The Alteration* (London, 1976). Philip Roth's classic *The Plot Against America* (New York, 2004) imagines a fascist and antisemitic United States following the election of Charles Lindbergh as U.S. president in 1940.

23   Geoffrey Parker, "If the Armada Had Landed," *History* 61 (1976), pp. 358–68.

24   Guido Morselli, *Past Conditional: A Retrospective Hypothesis* (London, 1989 [1975]).

25   Shulamit Volkov, *Walther Rathenau: Weimar's Fallen Statesman* (New Haven, CT, 2012).

26   Rodiek, *Erfundene Vergangenheit*, pp. 100–108; see also Susanne Kleinert, "Historiographie und fiktionale Geschichtdarstellung in Guido Morsellis 'Contro-passato prossimo,'" in Helene Harth et al., eds., *Konflikt der Diskurse: Zum Verhältnis von Literatur und Wissenschaft im modernen Italien* (Tübingen, 1991), pp. 231–48.

27   Victor Alba, *1936–1976: Historia de la II República Española* (Barcelona, 1976), discussed in Rodiek, *Erfundene Vergangenheit*, pp. 117–19.

28   Rodiek, *Erfundene Vergangenheit*, pp. 119–22, discussing Fernando Vizcaíno Casas, *Los rojos ganaron la guerra: Como hubiera podido ser el futuro — nuestro presente — si Franco pierde la guerra civil* (Barcelona, 1989), and Manuel Talens, "Ucronia," in *Venganzas* (Barcelona, 1994), pp. 25–34.

29　Barbara W. Tuchman, "If Mao Had Come to Washington: An Essay in Alternatives," *Foreign Affairs* 51 (1971–72), pp. 44–64. See also Rodiek, *Erfundene Vergangenheit*, p. 128.

30　Carr, *What Is History?* pp. 91–93.

31　Daniel Snowman, ed., *If I Had Been . . . Ten Historical Fantasies* (London, 1979).

32　Ibid., p. 2.

33　Ibid., pp. 4–5.

34　Ibid., pp. 6–8.

35　Niall Ferguson, ed., *Virtual History: Alternatives and Counterfactuals* (London, 1997), p. 12.

36　Ian Kershaw, *Popular Opinion and Political Dissent in the Third Reich: Bavaria 1933–1945* (Oxford, 1983), p. viii.

37　Snowman, *If I Had Been . . .* , pp. 3, 9.

38　Ibid., pp. 28, 70, 94–95.

39　Alexander Demandt, *History That Never Happened: A Treatise on the Question, What Would Have Happened If . . . ?* 3rd ed. (Jefferson, NC, 1993 [1984]), pp. 135–51.

40　John M.Merriman, ed., *For Want of a Horse: Choice and Chance in History* (Lexington, MA, 1985), p. x.

41　The following year saw another American collection, *Alternative Histories: Eleven Stories of the World as It Might Have Been*, ed. Charles G. Waugh and Martin H. Greenberg (New York, 1986), suggesting that the genre was starting already to come back into vogue. Compensatory fantasies about a Confederate victory in the American Civil War had already been parodied by the humorist James Thurber in his short story "If Grant Had Been Drinking at Appomattox" (available at numerous websites online).

42　Aviezer Tucker, review of Ferguson, *Virtual History*, in *History and Theory* 38, no. 2 (May 1999), pp. 254–76, here, pp. 265–66.

43　H. A. L. Fisher, *A History of Europe* (London, 1936), pp. v–vi.

44　Edward Hallett Carr, *From Napoleon to Stalin* (London, 1989), pp, 262–63 (interview with Perry Anderson).

45　Friedrich Meinecke, *Werke* (Munich, 1957–79), vol. 4, p. 261, quoted in Demandt, *History*, pp. 5–6.

46 Robert William Fogel, *Railroads and American Economic Growth: Essays in Econometric History* (Baltimore, MD, 1964). See also Stanley L. Engerman, "Counterfactuals and the New Economic History," *Inquiry* 23 (1980), pp. 157–72. For a defense of these procedures, see Eric Hobsbawm, *On History* (London, 1997), pp. 113–15.

47 Merriman, *For Want of a Horse*, p. ix.

48 "Historians Warming to Games of 'What If,'" *New York Times*, 7 January 1998; Martin Arnold, "The What Ifs That Fascinate," *New York Times*, 21 December 2000.

49 Rosenfeld, *The World Hitler Never Made*, pp. 4–11. See also his "Why Do We Ask 'What If?' Reflections on the Function of Alternate History," *History and Theory* 41, no. 4 (December, 2010). pp. 90–103.

50 Tristram Hunt, "Pasting Over the Past," *Guardian*, 7 April 2004.

51 Rosenfeld, *The World Hitler Never Made*, pp. 1–11. See also Mark A. Carnes, ed., *Past Imperfect: History According to the Movies* (New York, 1995), and Richard J. Evans, *In Defense of History*, 2nd ed., (London, 2001 [1997]).

52 Quoted in Philip E. Tetlock, Richard Ned Lebow, and Geoffrey Parker, eds., *Unmaking the West: "What-If?" Scenarios That Rewrite World History* (Ann Arbor, MI, 2000), pp. 14–16, 28–35 and notes.

53 Rosenfeld, *The World Hitler Never Made*, p. 11.

2. VIRTUAL HISTORY

1 Cowley, *More What If?*, p. xv.

2 Jeremy Black, *What If? Counterfactualism and the Problem of History* (London, 2008), pp. 6–7.

3 Andrew Roberts, *What Might Have Been: Leading Historians on Twelve "What Ifs" of History* (London, 2004), p. 2.

4 Benjamin Aldes Wurgaft, "The Uses of Walter: Walter Benjamin and the Counterfactual Imagination," *History and Theory* 49, no. 3 (October 2010), pp. 361–83; at p. 361.

5 Geoffrey Parker and Philip Tetlock, "Counterfactual Thought Experiments," in Tetlock, Lebow, and Parker, *Unmaking the West*, pp. 14–46, at p. 17.

6   Simon J. Kaye, "Challenging Certainty: The Utility and History of Counterfactualism," *History and Theory* 49, no. 1 (February 2010), pp, 38–57, at p. 38.

7   Merriman, *For Want of a Horse*, pp. ix–x.

8   Black, *What If?*, pp. 7–9.

9   Hunt, "Pasting Over the Past."

10   Carr, *What Is History?*, p. 95.

11   Roberts, *What Might Have Been*, p. 3.

12   Ferguson, *Virtual History*, pp. 53–55.

13   Eric Hobsbawm, *Primitive Rebels: Studies in Archaic Forms of Social Movement in the 19th and 20th Centuries* (Manchester, 1959); Edward Thompson, *The Making of the English Working Class* (London, 1991 [1963]), p. 12.

14   Edward Hallett Carr, *Socialism in One Country, 1924–1926*, vol. I (London, 1958), pp. 151–202 ("Personalities").

15   Ferguson, *Virtual History*, pp. 38–9.

16   Karl Marx, *Der achtzehnte Brumaire des Louis Bonaparte (1852)*, in *Karl Marx, Friedrich Engels, Ausgewählte Schriften in Zwei Bänden* (East Berlin, 1968), vol. 1, p. 226 (my translation).

17   Allan Megill, *Historical Knowledge, Historial Error: A Contemporary Guide to Practice* (Chicago, 2007), p. 152.

18   Fernand Braudel, *The Mediterranean and the Mediterranean World in the Age of Philip II*, 2 vols. (London, 1972–73 [1949]).

19   Fernand Braudel, *On History* (London, 1980), p. 80.

20   Ferguson, *Virtual History*, p. 87.

21   Herbert Butterfield, *The Whig Interpretation of History* (London, 1931).

22   Tucker, review of Ferguson, pp. 266–67.

23   Ferguson, *Virtual History*, pp. 61–62.

24   Ibid., p. 61.

25   See the classic critique in Pieter Geyl, *Debates with Historians* (London, 1962 [1955]), pp. 112–210.

26   Tucker, review of Ferguson, pp. 267–8, citing Maurice Mandelbaum, *The Anatomy of Historical Knowledge* (Baltimore, 1977), pp. 105–10.

27 Quoted in Ferguson, *Virtual History*, pp. 39–41.

28 Tucker, review of Ferguson, p. 268. Tucker's examples of *particular* counterfactuals that supposedly challenge *particular* theories are not counterfactuals but factuals.

29 Ferguson, *Virtual History*, pp. 64–67.

30 Tucker, review of Ferguson, p. 268; see also Evans, *In Defense of History*, pp. 68–69, 138–40, 148–49; and Hayden White, *Metahistory: The Historical Imagination in Nineteenth-Century Europe* (Baltimore, 1987).

31 See Paul M. Kennedy, *The Rise and Fall of the Great Powers* (London, 1987), and Lawrence Stone, *The Causes of the English Revolution 1529–1642* (London, 1975).

32 Tucker, review of Ferguson, p. 271.

33 Richard Ned Lebow, *Forbidden Fruit: Counterfactuals and International Relations* (Princeton, NJ, 2010), pp. 47–49.

34 Ferguson, *Virtual History*, p. 237.

35 Ibid., p. 279.

36 John Charmley, *Churchill: The End of Glory, A Political Biography* (London, 1992). See my discussion of this book in Richard J. Evans, *Rereading German History, 1800–1996: From Unification to Reunification* (London, 1996), pp. 204–12.

37 Alan Clark, "A Reputation Ripe for Revision," *The Times*, 2 January 1993. See also the excellent discussion in Rosenfeld, *The World Hitler Never Made*, pp. 83–86 and 88–89.

38 R. W. Johnson, "The Greatest Error of Modern History," *London Review of Books* 21, no. 4 (18 February 1999), pp. 7–8.

39 Ian Kershaw, *Hitler 1936–45: Nemesis* (London, 2000), pp. 369–80.

40 Roy Jenkins, *Churchill* (London, 2001), p. 608.

41 Paul Addison, "Churchill and the Price of Victory: 1939–1945," in Nick Tiratsoo, ed., *From Blitz to Blair: A New History of Britain Since 1939* (London, 1997), pp. 63–64.

42 Andrew Roberts, "Hitler's England: What if Germany Had Invaded Britain in May 1940?," in Ferguson, *Virtual History*, pp. 281–320, quote on p. 298.

43 C. J. Sansom, *Dominion* (London, 2012), pp. 571–93.

44 Holger H. Herwig, "Hitler Wins in the East but Germany Still Loses World War II," in Tetlock, Lebow, and Parker, *Unmaking the West*, pp. 323–62.

45 Sansom, *Dominion*, pp. 581–88.

46 John Lukacs, "What if Hitler Had Won the Second World War?," in David Wallechinsky, ed., *The People's Almanac*, vol. 2 (New York, 1978), pp. 396–98.

47 Paul Addison, *The Road to 1945: British Politics and the Second World War* (London, 1975).

48 Johannes Bulhof, "What If? Modality and History," *History and Theory* 38, no. 2 (May, 1999), pp. 145–68, at pp. 146–47.

49 Megill, *Historical Knowledge, Historial Error*, p. 152.

50 Martin Bunzl, "Counterfactual History: A User's Guide," *American Historical Review*, vol. 109 (2004), pp. 845–68.

51 Jon Elster, *Logic and Society: Contradictions and Possible Worlds* (New York, 1978).

52 Steven Lukes, "Elster on Counterfactuals," in *Inquiry: An Interdisciplinary Journal of Philosophy* 23, no. 2 (1980), pp. 145–55, at p. 153.

53 Carrère, *Le détroit de Behring*, p. 91 (my translation).

54 J. C. D. Clark, "British America: What If There Had Been no American Revolution?," in Ferguson, ed., *Virtual History*, pp. 125–74, here p. 174.

55 Ibid., p. 171.

56 Tetlock, Lebow, and Parker, *Unmaking the West*, p. 372.

57 Ferguson, *Virtual History*, p. 237.

58 Clark, "British America," p. 171.

59 Ibid., p. 174.

3. FUTURE FICTIONS

1 Jorge Semprún, *L'Algarabie* (Paris, 1981), pp. 109–15.

2 Rodiek, *Erfundene Vergangenheit*, pp. 15–24.

3 Tucker, review of Ferguson, p. 265.

4 Rosenfeld, *The World Hitler Never Made*, p. 518.

5 Ibid. See also Rodiek, *Erfundene Vergangenheit*, pp. 141–49 and 161–62.

6 Rosenfeld, *The World Hitler Never Made*, p. 518.

7 Henry Vollam Morton, *I, James Blunt* (Toronto, 1942), p. 3, quoted in Rosenfeld, *The World Hitler Never Made*, p. 39.

8 For Coward's play see Rodiek, *Erfundene Vergangenheit*, pp. 130–32.

9 Ibid., pp. 132–35. See also Carrère, *Le détroit de Behring*, p. 50.

10 Rosenfeld, *The World Hitler Never Made*, pp. 45–49.

11 Richard J. Evans, *Society and Politics in Wilhelmine Germany* (London, 1978), pp. 11–3.

12 Norman Longmate, *If Britain Had Fallen: The Real Nazi Occupation Plans* (London, 2004 [1972]), p. 109.

13 Ibid., pp. 107–108, 117–18, 116, 8.

14 Ibid., pp. 135–45, 173, 178–79, 186–206, 207–57, 258–62.

15 David Lampe, *The Last Ditch* (London, 1968), and Adrian Gilbert, *Britain Invaded* (London, 1990).

16 John Ramsden, *Don't Mention the War: The British and the Germans since 1890* (London, 2006), pp. 412–14. Rosenfeld (p. 71) attempts to sustain his thesis that there was a continuous process of "normalization" in British depictions of Germany and Nazism from the 1960s onward, with no backsliding or contradiction, by referring to a later, secondary source published in 2002 but does not take these poll data into account.

17 William Cash, *Against a Federal Europe: The Battle for Britain* (London, 1991), pp. 1, 71, 82.

18 John Charmley, "Why, Sadly, We Can Never Trust Germany," *Daily Mail*, 8 May 1995, p. 8.

19 See Andrew Bonnell, "Europhobia in the New Tory Historiography," in John Milfull, ed., *Britain in Europe: Prospects for Change* (Aldershot, 1999), 207–25.

20 Madeleine Bunting, *The Model Occupation: The Channel Islands under German Rule, 1940–1945* (London, 1995).

21 Roberts, "Hitler's England," p. 305.

22 Ibid., p. 317.

23 Owen Sheers, *Resistance* (London, 2007), p. 217.

24 Andrew Roberts, *The Aachen Memorandum* (London, 1995), pp. 10–11, 14–20, 25.

25 Ibid., pp. 9, 25.

26 Robert Harris, "Nightmare Landscape of Nazism Triumphant," *Sunday Times*, 10 May 1992, section 2, p. 1, quoted in Rosenfeld, *The World Hitler Never Made*, p. 423, n. 187. Rosenfeld (n. 188) notes that Harris distanced himself from the view that other features of the EU resembled a Nazi-run Europe, but the fact remains that the novel shared many features of the anti-German British Euroscepticism of the 1990s.

27 Rosenfeld, *The World Hitler Never Made*, p. 87. See also Rodiek, *Erfundene Vergangenheit*, pp. 150–152; and Philip Purser, "Hitler's Common Market," *London Review of Books*, 6 August 1991, p. 22.

28 Sansom, *Dominion*, pp. 578, 588.

29 Ibid., pp. 584–85.

30 Timothy W. Mason, *Social Policy in the Third Reich: The Working Class and the "National Community"* (Providence, RI, 1993), p. 7. See also, as a contrast, Niall Ferguson, "What Might Have Happened," *Times Literary Supplement*, 19 September 2007.

31 Richard J. Evans, *The Third Reich at War* (New York, 2009), pp. 332–33.

32 Rosenfeld, *World Hitler Never Made*, pp. 15–18, 22–23, 193–94, etc.

33 Ibid., p. 33, for an example.

34 Ibid., pp. 199–245, 259.

35 Bill Niven, *Facing the Nazi Past: United Germany and the Legacy of the Third Reich* (London, 2002), offers a useful introduction.

36 Peter Novick, *The Holocaust and Collective Memory: The American Experience* (New York, 1999), pp. 127–45.

37 Rosenfeld, *The World Hitler Never Made*, pp. 227–31.

38 W. Hugh Thomas, *Doppelgängers: The Truth About the Bodies in the Bunker* (London, 1995); also his *The Murder of Rudolf Hess* (London, 1979); and *SS-1: The Unlikely Death of Heinrich Himmler* (London, 2001).

39 See Deborah Lipstadt, *Denying the Holocaust: The Growing Assault on Truth and Memory* (New York, 1994), and Richard J. Evans, *Telling Lies about Hitler: The Holocaust, History, and the David Irving Trial* (London, 2002).

40 http://www.publicpolicypolling.com/pdf/2011/PPP_Release, accessed 11 April 2013.

41 Philip K Dick, *The Man in the High Castle* (London, 2001 [1962]), pp. 246–47.

42 Keith Roberts, *Pavane* (London, 1968); Kingsley Amis, *The Alteration* (London, 1976).

43 Rodiek, *Erfundene Vergangenheit*, p. 42. See also Jörg Helbig, *Der parahistorische Roman: Ein literaturhistorischer und gattungstypologischer Beitrag zur Allotopieforschung* (Frankfurt am Main, 1988), and Eric B. Henriet, *L'histoire révisité: L'uchronie dans toutes ses formes* (Paris, 1999).

44 Christian Goeschel, *Suicide in Nazi Germany* (Oxford, 2009).

45 See Karen Hellekson, *The Alternate History: Refiguring Historical Time* (Kent, OH, 2001); and Ian Watson and Ian Whates, eds., *The Mammoth Book of Alternate Histories* (New York, 2010).

4. POSSIBLE WORLDS

1 Nathaniel Hawthorne, "P's Correspondence," in *Mosses from an Old Manse* (New York, 1846).

2 Hilary Mantel, *Wolf Hall* (London, 2009); also, *Bring up the Bodies* (London, 2012).

3 See I. F. Clarke, *Voices Prophesying War: Future Wars, 1763–3749* (London, 1992).

4 Rodiek, *Erfundene Vegangenheit*, p. 48.

5 Black, *What If?*, p. 188.

6 Tucker, review of Ferguson, p. 276.

7 Black, *What If?*, pp. 91, 188–90.

8 Tucker, review of Ferguson, p. 274.

9 Roberts, *What Might Have Been*, flap text of paperback edition (2005).

10 Tetlock, Lebow, and Parker, *Unmaking the West*, p. 335.

11 Dominic Sandbrook, "What If . . . Egypt Had Ruled Over Us," *New Statesman*, 2 December 2010; "What If . . . William Hadn't Conquered," *New Statesman*, 1 July 2010; "What If . . . Henry V

Had Lived On," *New Statesman*, 6 January 2011; "What If . . . Little Prince Hal Had Lived," *New Statesman*, 3 February 2011; "What If . . . Reformation Had Failed," *New Statesman*, 8 July 2010. Dawkins is of course the militant English atheist Richard Dawkins, author of *The God Delusion*; Muggeridge, who stands in for General Franco in an imagined English setting, was the acerbic journalist Malcolm Muggeridge.

12   Dominic Sandbrook, "What If . . . Britain Was Still a Republic," *New Statesman*, 4 November 2010.

13   Ferguson, "Afterword: A Virtual History, 1646–1996," in *Virtual History*, pp. 416–40.

14   Ferguson, *Virtual History*, pp. 14–17.

15   Tucker, review of Ferguson, p. 276.

16   Roberts, *What Might Have Been*, pp. 15–58.

17   Ferguson, *Virtual History*, pp. 91–124. Robert Cowley's contribution to Roberts's volume (pp. 59–78) is not true counterfactual history because, while describing how one very small and specific incident might have altered the course of the War of American Independence, it does not go into the consequences of this. Amanda Foreman (pp. 92–104), suggesting that the war that threatened between Britain and the United States in 1861 might not have been averted, is, like Cowley, more interested in the mechanics of how history took another turn than in the consequences of the alternative turn taken.

18   Jonathan Haslam, "Stalin's War or Peace: What If the Cold War Had Been Avoided?," in Ferguson, *Virtual History*, pp. 348–67.

19   Roberts, *What Might Have Been*, pp. 79–133.

20   Ibid., 166–88.

21   Black, *What If?*, p. 10.

22   Tetlock, Lebow, and Parker, *Unmaking the West*, pp. 241–322; William H. McNeill, "What If Pizarro Had Not Found Potatoes in Peru?," in Cowley, *More What If?*, pp. 413–27, mostly actually devoted to a straightforward account of the actual influence of the potato in Europe.

23   Hunt, "Pasting Over the Past."

24 Lubomir Dolezel, *Possible Worlds of Fiction and History: The Postmodern Stage* (Baltimore, MD, 2010), p. 122.

25 Hawthorn, *Plausible Worlds*, pp. 39–80.

26 Joel Mokyr, "King Kong and Cold Fusion: Counterfactual Analysis of the History of Technology," in Tetlock, Lebow, and Parker, *Unmaking the West*, pp. 277–322, at p. 311.

27 Niall Ferguson, *Civilization: The West and the Rest* (London, 2011).

28 Tucker, review of Ferguson, p. 275.

29 Tetlock, Lebow, and Parker, *Unmaking the West*, pp. 264–65.

30 Henry A. Turner, Jr., *Hitler's Thirty Days to Power: January, 1933* (New York, 1996), p. 168.

31 Tetlock, Lebow, and Parker, *Unmaking the West*, pp. 264–65.

32 Richard J. Evans, *The Coming of the Third Reich* (New York, 2003), pp. 301–308.

33 Megill, *Historical Knowledge, Historical Error*, p. 151.

34 Ibid., pp. 153–54.

35 Ibid., p. 152–55.

36 Tucker, review of Ferguson, p. 270.

37 Ibid.

38 Bulhof, "What If?," pp. 155–56; Daniel Jonah Goldhagen, *Hitler's Willing Executioners: Ordinary Germans and the Holocaust* (New York, 1996), p. 6.

39 Bunzl, "Counterfactual History," p. 855.

40 Ibid., p. 857.

41 Ibid.

42 Sansom, *Dominion*, p. 589.

43 Thus the Soviet Union was already producing more than three times as many tanks than Germany in 1943, a disparity not reduced by Speer's rationalization measures: see Evans, *The Third Reich at War*, pp. 332–33.

44 Tucker, review of Ferguson, pp. 268–71; citing Yemima Ben-Menachem, "Historical Contingency," *Ratio* 10 (1997), pp. 99–107.

45 In Cowley, *More What If?*, pp. 279–90.

46 Herwig, in Tetlock, Lebow, and Parker, *Unmaking the West*, pp. 323–60.

47 Parker and Tetlock, in ibid., p. 367.

48 Goldstone, in ibid., pp. 168–96.

49 Pestana, in ibid., pp. 367, 200.

50 Robert J. W. Evans, *Rudolf II and His World: A Study in Intellectual History, 1576–1612* (Oxford, 1973).

51 See the interesting, if somewhat inconclusive discussion in Lebow, *Forbidden Fruit*, pp. 69–102 ("Franz Ferdinand Found Alive: World War I Unnecessary"). For yet another example of wishful thinking in connection with the survival of Franz Ferdinand in 1914, see Demandt, *History*, pp. 104–7.

52 Hobsbawm, *On History*, pp. 245–46.

53 Herwig, "Hitler Wins," p. 352.

54 See the brilliant cultural history by Michael Saler, *As If: Modern Enchantment and the Literary Prehistory of Virtual Reality* (New York, 2012).

55 Tetlock, Lebow, and Parker, *Unmaking the West*, p. 389.

56 Max Weber, "Kritische Studien auf dem Gebiet der kulturwissenschaftlichen Logik" (1906), in *Gesammelte Aufsätze zur Wissenschaftslehre* (1968), p. 275, cited in Demandt, *History*, p. 14.

57 Rosenfeld, "Why Do We Ask 'What If?'" p. 90.

58 Wurgaft, "The Uses of Walter," p. 361.

59 Friedrich Nietzsche, *Werke*, vol. 4, part 1, p. 132, cited in Demandt, *History*, p. 1.

60 Walther Rathenau, *Die neue Wirtschaft* (Berlin, 1918), p. 82, cited in Rodiek, *Erfundene Vergangenheit*, p. 100.

INDEX

Actium, Battle of: won by Mark
Antony, 2, 98
Adamson, John, 32–33, 103, 114
Addison, Paul, 52, 57, 62
Alba, Victor, 15
Alexander the Great: conquers
Rome, 2
Allen, Louis, 20
Allende, Salvador: avoids coup,
20–21
America, United States of: becomes another Canada, 23; defeated by Confederacy, 10–12,
23, 90; destroys British Empire, 49–55; does not invade
Afghanistan, 60; drops atomic
bomb on Germany, 72, 113; existence avoided, 1, 19, 21, 23, 61,
99, 101, 109–10; friendship with
Germany, 13; neutral in World
War II, 50; no Civil War, 1, 23;
peace with Nazi Germany, 79;
preempted by Spanish con-
quest, 14; war with Nazi Germany, 80–81, 100, 104; writers
dominate counterfactualism,
66, 96
Anglo-Saxons: rule England into
twentieth century, 98
Antarctica: Nazis in, 87
Argentina: Hitler escapes to, 85,
91; wins Falklands War, 100–101

Armada, Spanish (1588): fails, 65;
makes no difference, 103; succeeds, 1, 2, 13, 22, 89, 106
atomic bomb: American, 118;
dropped on Germany, 72, 113;
dropped on London and Chicago, 68; Nazi, 118; used by partisans, 117–18
Auschwitz, 72, 76, 83, 86, 121
Austria, Don John of: marries
Mary Queen of Scots, 10–11
Austria-Hungary: conquers Italy
and France, 14; and World
War I, 47, 58, 122

Battle of Britain: RAF loses, 71
Beauharnais, Joséphine de, 4
Beckett, Francis, 97
Bismarck, Otto von, 11, 40, 75, 113
Black, Conrad, 104
Black, Jeremy, 28, 31–33, 37, 94–95,
106
Blakemore, Harold, 20
Bonaparte, Napoleon: chance in
career, 40; conquers world, 3–6;
decides not to conquer world,
6, 8; defeated in 1812, 104; dis-
regards constraints, 46–47;
loses Battle of Waterloo, 65;
survives to 1845, 92; wins Battle
of Waterloo, 1, 8–9, 33, 107
Boston Tea Party: called off, 23

feated, 23, 65, 98, 109–10,
121–22
Goldhagen, Daniel Jonah, 117
Goldstone, Jack, 121–22
Gorbachev, Mikhail, 104
Gore, Albert, Jr., U.S. president, 1,
60, 96, 105–107
Greece, 10–11, 53
Grey, Edward, 47–48, 59, 62, 95,
106, 122
Guedalla, Philip, 9–11
Gunpowder Plot (1605): fails, 65;
succeeds, 41, 103, 106–107

Halifax, Lord: prime minister, 49,
51, 97, 121
Hansig, Ron T., 84, 88
Harris, Robert, 78–81
Haslam, Jonathan, 104
Hastings, Battle of: Harold wins,
98
Hawkins, Martin, 68
Hawthorn, Geoffrey, 108
Hawthorne, Nathaniel, 92
Heath, Edward, 96
Heffer, Simon, 105
Henry V (king of England): rules
France, 98
Herwig, Holger, 54, 57, 62, 97, 121,
124
Heseltine, Michael: prime minis-
ter, 105
Hess, Rudolf, 49–52, 84, 90
Heywood, Joseph, 83
Himmler, Heinrich, 84, 90
Hindenburg, Paul von, 14–15, 111
Hitler, Adolf: cannot end war, 81;
commits suicide, 90; defeats

USSR, 52–53; did not kill Jews,
86; did not want to survive war,
90; dies after war, 119; disre-
gards constraints, 46–47; does
not come to power, 102; ends
war, 80–81; escapes to South
America, 83–86, 89–91; few
German counterfactuals about,
66; intends war, 119–20; invades
UK, 53, 76–81; killed in 1930, 1,
25; killed in 1944, 118; killed in
World War I, 115–16; loses war,
113; not tried for crimes, 90;
offers peace to UK, 51; replaced
by double, 84, 92; *Second Book*,
80; shocked by Hess's flight,
51; supported by Germans, 13;
stalemate on Eastern Front, 50,
53, 80–81, 119; survives war, 90;
tried for crimes, 83; triumph
in 1933 not inevitable, 40–41,
89–90, 110–11; wins World
War II, 67, 124. *See also* Germany
Hoare, Samuel: collaborationist
prime minister, 71, 76, 121
Hobsbawm, Eric, 34–35, 122
Holocaust, 1, 13, 48, 50, 75–76,
78–80, 82, 117 (*see also* Auschwitz); denial of, 44, 86–87
Holy Roman Empire: conquers
Britain and France, 99–100; not
abolished, 99, 101
Hugo, Victor, 1, 5, 8
Hunt, Tristram, 29, 33–34, 107
Hutchinson, Governor: prevents
Boston Tea Party, 23
Hynek, J. Allen, 87